Ellen & Derek Jameson

Siobhán's Miracle

They told us she had weeks to live. Then the most amazing miracle happened...

JOHN BLAKE

Published by John Blake Publishing Ltd,
3 Bramber Court, 2 Bramber Road,
London W14 9PB, England

www.blake.co.uk

First published in hardback in 2008

ISBN: 978 1 84454 566 7

British Library Cataloguing-in-Publication Data:

A catalogue record for this book is available from the British Library.

Design by www.envydesign.co.uk

Printed in the UK by CPI William Clowes Beccles NR34 7TL

1 3 5 7 9 10 8 6 4 2

Papers used by John Blake Publishing are natural, recyclable products
made from wood grown in sustainable forests. The manufacturing processes
conform to the environmental regulations of the country of origin.

Acknowledgements

Dedicated with grateful thanks to the relatives, friends and colleagues who were more than happy to contribute their memories of Professor Kilfeather for inclusion in *Siobhan's Miracle*. These pages reflect the love and admiration that surrounded her at every turn. Thanks too to John Blake, editor Daniel Bunyard and everyone at John Blake Publishing for so readily devoting their time and talent to make it possible for us to tell the story of this remarkable woman. Special thanks to Medbh McGuckian for her splendid poetry, To Dr Clair Wills and The Guardian for Siobhan's obituary and to Gary Eason, who provided most of the photographs.

Who will be there
At that moment, beside her
When time becomes sacred
And her voice becomes an opera,
And the solitude is removed
From her body, as if my hand
Had been held in some invisible place?
MEDBH MCGUCKIAN

Siobhán Kilfeather

Forthright champion of Irish women writers

Loved for her sharpness and wit, and occasionally feared for her forthrightness, Siobhán Kilfeather, who has died of cancer aged 49, was an expert on 18th-century Ireland whose work helped transform the study of the history of sexuality in Ireland. Few scholars brought such grace and intelligence to their work, combining erudition and rigour with warmth and unparalleled generosity to others. She was much loved as a teacher whose standards encouraged excellence in her students, many of whom went on to teach in British, Irish and US universities.

Her research interests ranged from 18th-century and romantic literature to gender studies, Irish studies, the Gothic, postcolonialism, cinema and intersections between literature and the visual arts. She published critical editions of Maria Edgeworth and Louisa M Alcott, and her Dublin: A Cultural and Literary History was published in 2005.

She was best known as an editor of The Field Day Anthology of Irish Writing, Volumes 4 and 5 (2003). The first three volumes of the anthology had been attacked from several quarters. And some of the most bitter complaints were sparked by its perceived neglect of the female contribution to Irish literature and culture. Siobhán's critical but measured interventions in this argument helped set the agenda for the two subsequent volumes, entirely devoted to women's writing.

Yet she had little patience with wishy-washy or sentimental versions of gender and identity politics. I recall one of our long meetings in which the eight editors tried to thrash out exactly what we meant by gender and sexuality. Siobhán was explaining why she thought it was important to include writing by men in an anthology dedicated to women writers, part of her insistence on the primacy of real lives and practices over abstract ideas of identity. She waved an impatient arm at our rather dry conceptualisations: "What I want to know is, were they fist-fucking in the 18th century?" she would say.

Siobhán was born in Belfast, daughter of John and Rene Kilfeather. John was a shy civil servant whose real passion was literature. Their home was a shambling, bohemian meeting point for the poet John Hewitt and his socialist literary

Siobhán Kilfeather combined erudition and rigour with warmth and generosity

circle. Kilfeather relatives remember a house overflowing with books. Siobhán was encouraged to form opinions about her reading from a very early age.

In 1976 she was the first pupil from her school, Rathmore, in Belfast to gain a Cambridge scholarship – to Selwyn College. Fellow students recall how she would sit in lectures with neither pen nor paper to hand, while they furiously scribbled notes. "If it's important, you'll remember it," she would say.

She then worked in London and Rome but returned to Belfast in 1980, one of the most acute periods of the Troubles, the time of IRA hunger strikes and dirty protests. Siobhán spent two years involved in cultural politics and creative writing in Belfast, before winning a scholarship to take a PhD at Princeton University in New Jersey. A post in the school of English at Columbia University in New York followed.

In 1992 she married Peter Jameson, and settled in Shropshire, from where she commuted to Sussex University and her post as an English lecturer. Their beloved children, Constance and Oscar, were born in 1995 and 1997. In 2004 the family returned to Belfast, where Siobhán joined the school of English at Queen's University, committed to developing the study of Irish literary culture in the wake of the political settlement.

Seven years ago she struggled with and seemed to have beaten melanoma, in part through her determination to spend more time with her children, who were then only two and four. When the cancer returned some months ago she accepted it with equal bravery and determination.

A few weeks before she died, Siobhán said to me that one of the things she was surprised to find herself regretting was that she might not get to find out what happened to Harry Potter. Such oblique and funny asides were characteristic of her. It was not so much about the waste of time reading the first six volumes, but her intense engagement with plot. Narrative was fundamental to her worldview. She was fascinated by the way that the formal requirements of a plot and storyline both ground us in a particular past – for her a past rooted in Catholic Ireland – and at the same time create the tensions and possibilities for unknown futures.

She is survived by her husband, children, and by her brother Myles.

Clair Wills

Siobhán Marie Kilfeather, academic, born August 9 1957; died April 7 2007

Contents

Chapter One

Give Me More Time

Siobhán's life is spelled out neatly in Dr Clair Wills's obituary in the *Guardian*, but diplomatically she omits any mention of the extraordinary Damascene happening at Lourdes seven years previously. As stepmother of Siobhán's husband Peter, I was alongside her on that cheerless February day in the French Pyrenees and again when she passed away peacefully in Belfast on Easter Saturday, 7 April 2007. My memories of the occasion are poignant.

The noonday sun was shining brightly in a cloudless blue sky outside the window of the young patient's room on the third floor of the Cancer Centre at Belfast City Hospital. The last rites had already been administered. Siobhán Kilfeather gave one last deep sigh. Peter hugged her and I held her hand as she slipped away after a mercifully short battle with cancer.

The sun was still shining when we laid her to rest beside her mother in a small graveyard in the shadow of a hillside in a village called Hope in Shropshire. Johnny Cash sang 'We'll Meet Again' over loudspeakers at the funeral in Shrewsbury Cathedral.

Dr Siobhán Kilfeather was Professor of English and Irish Literature at Queen's University, Belfast, a graduate of Cambridge University and Princeton University and a former tutor at Columbia University, New York. In August 2007 she would have turned fifty.

Constance, the image of her mother, with her thick, deep brown, wavy hair and piercing blue eyes, celebrated her twelfth birthday at her mother's bedside on 5 April 2007. The younger child, Oscar, handsome, tall, football-loving, would turn ten in September of that year.

Siobhán did not cry 'Why me?' or rage against the cancer which cruelly ravaged her body between Christmas Eve 2006 and her death the following Easter. Siobhán knew she was living on borrowed time. Thanks to her gentle Irish charm, faith in God and belief in a mother's love, she had entered a holy pact with the Blessed Mother of Jesus. Her fervent prayer had been that she be granted time to see her children grow to an age where they would know and remember her.

By her devotion and faith, she won an extra seven years of life. That was how long it took from the time doctors first warned they could not guarantee her survival until eventually the cancerous melanomas which ravaged her body took her life.

Those seven vital years began as we knelt at the feet of the statue of the Queen of Heaven in the shrine at Lourdes.

'Hail Mary, full of Grace.' Siobhán chanted the first line of the universal prayer to Mary. Then, with hands outstretched and eyes full of fire, she beseeched the statue. 'Holy Mary, Mother of God,' she prayed aloud, 'you know better than anyone on earth the love a mother has for her children. Surely you won't deprive my babies of their mother. They need me. I beg you; find it in your heart to give me more time. Let me see them grow up a bit first – then I'll be ready.'

Siobhán and I looked at each other with tears in our eyes. We lit candles in the flower-filled grotto where the Virgin Mary is said to have appeared to young Bernadette Soubirous 150 years ago.

It was February 2000 and the Pyrenean weather

was still bitterly cold. Although she was tired after our flight from London that day, by evening Siobhán declared she was well enough to walk in a candlelight procession with thousands of other pilgrims celebrating the Feast of Our Lady.

Before her illness Siobhán had been a vibrant, energetic young woman who loved walking and keeping fit. Now she walked painfully slowly and her breathing was laboured. The cancer had reached her lungs. She took my arm as we struggled to keep up with the other worshippers moving reverently through the grotto gardens in procession, praying the rosary and singing hymns.

We took comfort in the familiar and much-loved words of the hymns to Mary, Queen of Heaven, Ocean Star and Hail Glorious Mary from our Catholic schooldays. Suddenly Siobhán turned to me and with complete conviction declared, 'I felt a shift inside my body today. I believe the cancer has left me. Mary has answered my prayer. She says I am to be allowed some more time with my wee ones.'

In those dark and uncertain days Siobhán and all who loved her would have settled for any extension to her life, which had been under threat since the cancer was diagnosed a year earlier. Seven years would have seemed like a lifetime – but that is what she was granted.

The following day I followed Siobhán into the freezing-cold waters of the plunge baths where nuns with strong hands and gentle hearts helped the faithful immerse themselves in the healing waters.

Siobhán walked purposefully down the stone steps to immerse herself. I followed, trying to hide the shock that swept over me as the thin, modesty-covering gown she had been provided with slipped from her shoulders. I had never before seen her operation scars. Now I shall never forget the livid wounds on her back where surgeons had twice removed cancerous growths.

We flew home from Lourdes on Sunday and two days later Siobhán and her husband Peter were due to attend the Royal Marsden Hospital in London, where she was to undergo what she had been told would be 'very aggressive' chemotherapy.

Chapter Two

Fear and Faith

The all too familiar journey from her home in Shropshire to the Royal Marsden over and registration complete, Siobhán had one urgent question for one of the specialist nurses she knew from previous visits. 'A friend has baked me some hash cookies,' she confided. 'What is the received medical wisdom on the healing properties of marijuana?' The nurse confirmed what Siobhán had already read on the Internet: that marijuana could help the patient to relax during the therapeutic process. Even more importantly, it was not known to have any detrimental effect on the chemotherapy she was about to undergo.

The nurse showed Siobhán to her bed in a small

ward. Peter watched as his wife unpacked her suitcase and neatly folded her specially bought pyjamas at the bottom of the bed. Then Siobhán stowed the rest of her belongings in the bedside locker and waited to be taken to X-ray.

With Siobhán signed in, Peter was leaving, having been reassured that she was in good hands with the hospital's ever-capable and compassionate nurses. In a small side ward Siobhán was about to change into a hospital gown by her bed. As Peter walked away along the corridor she called him on her mobile, urging him to come straight back.

The nursing staff wanted him to attend a hastily arranged conference in a side office. Siobhán clutched Peter's hand, her face ashen. She was dreading the prospect of being told that things were even worse than they had been led to expect. Perhaps they could not treat her.

'The Room of Death,' she said dramatically. 'I knew it, I'm too ill even to be given any treatment. I'm going to die. I can see it in their faces. They can't look me in the eye.'

Though no less fearful, Peter tried to reassure her. 'That's their professionally inscrutable persona. Noncommittal – you're not supposed to be able to read their expressions.'

After a few minutes, which Peter remembers felt

like hours, the couple were shown into a room. There on the clinical lightboxes were Siobhán's X-rays. A clinical team of half a dozen people had gathered: doctors, nurses and a radiologist. Sensing her distress, a young registrar spoke kindly to Siobhán, saying simply, 'You'll soon feel better.'

The previous year Siobhán had undergone a series of radical operations and chemotherapy sessions. These interventions seemed to have been successful and she had been kept under observation with a twice-yearly check-up. A watching brief, the radiologist had called it, playing down the seriousness of the possible malignancy in the lungs.

'As the time of the six-monthly appointment approached, Siobhán had been getting more and more wound up,' remembers Peter. 'She desperately craved the reassurance that only the medical staff could give her that all was well.'

But, determined to get on with a normal family Christmas for the sake of their children, Siobhán and Peter had tried to put aside doubts and fears. 'We'll deal with it if and when the time comes,' they had told each other. Besides, Constance and Oscar, then four and two, were too young to be aware there was anything wrong. Siobhán and Peter were determined to keep it that way.

By the time of the next scheduled appointment,

Siobhán had begun to experience breathing difficulties. At that examination the radiologist had confirmed her worst fears. X-rays showed that minuscule discrepancies observed on her previous visit had intensified. Secondary cancer in the lungs was extremely bad news and the medical team warned Siobhán that she was facing an aggressive course of chemotherapy. She would need to be admitted as an in-patient while the chemical cocktail was administered and monitored.

One immediate disappointment was that having been part of a clinical trial for the new cancer wonder drug, Interferon, she was now taken off the treatment. Clinical trials are monitored under strict medical conditions to assess their potential effectiveness to the largest number of patients. Once the standard norm is compromised – as in Siobhán's apparent lung irregularities – the trial becomes worthless. She pleaded in vain for the trial to be allowed to continue. In any event, she was informed, the Interferon might react negatively with the new chemical regime she was about to undergo.

Using the intervening weeks to arrange time off work and to arrange childcare, Siobhán started to prepare for the inevitable period of incapacitation. The University of Sussex granted her an open-ended leave of absence from her duties as a lecturer in English Literature and Feminist Studies.

It was at this time that Siobhán had accepted a family invitation to undertake her pilgrimage to the Holy Shrine of the Blessed Mary at Lourdes. By great good fortune, the visit had coincided with the Feast of Our Blessed Lady – Mary's Feast Day – on 13 February.

'Siobhán called several times from Lourdes,' Peter explains, 'and she certainly sounded spiritually refreshed. Her attitude was hopeful and positive.

'Strangely enough, she never actually suggested that she might have been granted a miracle or a reprieve. It was more that she felt energised and inspired. Most important of all – a priceless gift – she declared herself no longer afraid.'

And now, a few days after Siobhán's return from Lourdes, she and Peter waited as the radiologist stepped across the room to the X-ray plates. His first words sent a wave of shock and relief through Siobhán, who was shaking by this time. He came straight to the point. 'There are no abnormalities on the X-rays. Whatever appeared to be there – is there no longer. No treatment is required.'

Siobhán and Peter clung to each other as the radiologist continued. 'Back in December we spotted a small lesion on the lungs – one month later the abnormality was the size of a walnut. By now we expected to be examining irregular cells the size of a grapefruit. Instead, there is nothing to be seen. The abnormalities have disappeared.'

Peter shook his head in disbelief. Siobhán, stunned, shocked and too relieved to ask for further explanation, stammered, 'Am I cured? I've just come back from Lourdes.'

Before anyone could whisper the word 'miracle', the leader of the medical team smiled indulgently and said, 'Let's not go down that path. Just be glad that for today you're free to go home. We'll keep you under observation, but try not to get your hopes up too high, too soon.'

Not wishing to tempt fate by staying any longer than necessary, Siobhán almost ran to her bed, repacked her suitcase and tore out of the door into the street.

'Only when we were out in the fresh air, did we dare to breathe again,' says a still bemused Peter. 'It was as if a huge weight had been lifted from our minds. Who could deny that something profound had happened.'

As they walked away from the hospital hand in hand, Peter let out a sigh of relief and Siobhán said a prayer of thanks. Hailing a taxi, they went to the London address where their children, Constance and

Oscar, were being taken care of while Siobhán underwent treatment.

To this day Peter admits to no religious faith. Even so, back then he had been willing to believe a miracle might just be possible if he wished hard enough. Welcoming Siobhán back from her pilgrimage to Lourdes, he had said a silent prayer.

And now, it seemed, the cancer was vanquished.

On the phone to us that evening Siobhán was cautiously optimistic. 'I'm still in shock,' she confessed, 'but so far, so good. The Blessed Mary has answered my prayer.'

She certainly never doubted that she had been spared by the grace of God. She never ceased giving grateful thanks for her reprieve and returned to the faith of her childhood with a renewed fervour.

When you have been so close and stared death in the face, life itself becomes more precious than ever. Siobhán set about completing all the things she thought would be denied to her for ever.

Siobhán embraced life with new vigour. Not knowing how much time she had been granted, she was determined to make every second count. Over the next five years, under constant monitoring from the Royal Marsden, the cancer did not return. Siobhán was given the all-clear.

She returned to her post at the University of

Sussex, where she had worked since 1991, and completed a ten-year research project with fellow academics. This dedicated scholarship produced the final two volumes of *The Field Day Anthology of Irish Writing*, already the foremost work on writing by and about Irish women.

Then, in 2004, Siobhán was appointed to the position that she had coveted for years, Professor of Irish Studies at her alma mater, Queen's University, Belfast.

The family gladly moved across the Irish Sea from their home in Shropshire and Siobhán was immensely proud when eleven-year-old Constance was accepted as a pupil at Rathmore Grammar, the school from which she herself had launched a high-profile transatlantic academic career. Oscar, two years younger, was installed in a good, football-playing school and husband Peter closed down his public relations company to begin a degree in film studies at Queen's.

Happily settled in their Belfast home with a new black Labrador puppy and three cats, they felt life could not have been better. Then, on Christmas Eve 2006, came the devastating news. The cancer had returned.

Peter sounded scared when he phoned us. He waited until the children, excitedly anticipating a visit from Father Christmas, had gone to bed. Not quite asleep, they could be heard in the background loudly debating the question of Father Christmas's existence. Their voices carried across the corridor from bedroom to bedroom. 'I'm too old to believe in Father Christmas,' called Oscar crossly. 'If you don't believe in him, he won't come,' his big sister Constance warned him.

Peter called up the stairs, 'I'm on the phone to Nanny and Granddad. If you don't go to sleep Father Christmas won't be coming to either of you.'

We all laughed. Then he dropped the bombshell. 'Siobhán hasn't been too well. She has had some tests. She's going back to the Royal Marsden next week.' Siobhán took the phone. 'Don't worry,' she tried to reassure us. 'It's early stages. They don't even know yet if the spots they can see on their X-rays really are cancer or scars from old operations.'

'Merry Christmas – we'll talk tomorrow.'

As I put the phone down, my husband Derek and I looked at each other with tears in our eyes. We feared the worst. I went to my office and lit one of the candles we had brought back from Lourdes.

'Dear God,' I prayed, 'give us all strength.'

Chapter Three

Under Siobhán's Spell

Peter Jameson and Siobhán met in the summer of 1989. At that time Siobhán was living in America and maintaining a transatlantic relationship with long-time boyfriend Gary Eason, the couple having first met as undergraduates at Cambridge University. Gary subsequently joined a graduate training scheme on the *Wolverhampton Express & Star*. Siobhán was offered a place on the same course but declined.

'I pictured myself having a glamorous career in London or New York,' she used to say. 'Wolverhampton held no attraction for me – though I did enjoy visiting friends in the Shropshire countryside at weekends and for holidays.'

Peter was working as a sub-editor on the *Wolverhampton Express & Star*'s sister paper, the *Shropshire Star*. Gary and he became firm friends and drinking buddies.

At Dulwich College, where he had finished his education, Peter had found a degree of fame or notoriety as winner of a mock election. He swept the board in student votes with a creation of his own, the Punky Lazar Independence Party, an offshoot of his rock group, the Punky Lazar Hot Five.

Having gone against his father's wishes by refusing to wear the school's signature headgear – a straw boater – Peter brought further disappointment when he left with poor A level results, having previously won a scholarship to Dulwich. He turned his back on the option of university and instead went straight on a journalist training course. So it came about that he was an experienced newspaperman while still in his early twenties, perhaps emulating his father, Derek Jameson, who became editor of four national newspapers.

On one of Siobhán's early visits to Shropshire, Gary invited Peter for a meal and to meet his girlfriend. Peter fell under Siobhán's spell. 'She made a huge impact on me,' he recalls. 'She was beautiful, intelligent and funny.'

Sadly Peter's impact on Siobhán was less favourable. With remarkable candour he reveals the answer she gave when asked her first impressions of him. 'He was sloppy,' Siobhán confided. 'He would come to dinner, drink too much and fall asleep at the table. That happened almost every time he visited us. I was not impressed.'

Obviously Siobhán's view mellowed with time. Twenty years later, in the foreword to a guide book she wrote on Dublin, she paid homage to 'my jazz-playing, football-loving, whisky-drinking, star-gazing Jewish husband'.

When she visited Shropshire from London and later from her teaching post at New York's Columbia University, Siobhán would stay in the small flat Gary rented in the new town of Telford. Friends remember that she brought her own brand of exotica and Celtic magic to the place.

Her dress style was individualistic and evoked a bygone era, casual yet eye-catching. She favoured vintage rather than fashionable and loved clothes with an unexpected twist. One sombre black embroidered coat opened to reveal a shocking-pink silk lining.

Peter admits to being besotted with Siobhán from their first meeting. 'Although I deliberately engineered being in her company at every opportunity, she was the girlfriend of my best friend so I was not crass enough to make a move. Though

I never hid my feelings for her, I disguised a quiet, desperate kind of unrequited love in a public display of flirting, joking and self-deprecation.'

Peter and Siobhán shared a passion for the cinema and when the couple moved to Belfast near the end of Siobhán's life, Peter fulfilled a long-held ambition. He became a mature student and studied for a degree at the Film School at Queen's University.

With his romantic cinematographer's vision Peter offers a perfect picture of his late wife. 'In my mind's eye,' he says, 'I have this wonderful soft-focus image of Siobhán sitting in the flower-filled summer garden of a cottage in Wales. She was wearing a long, flowing pastel-coloured dress; her dark, wavy hair was tumbling over her shoulders. Lounging back in a wicker chair, she was sipping a mint julep.

'How could I not be in love with her?'

In time it became clear to Siobhán and Gary and their friends that their relationship was heading for the rocks. Whenever the couple had one of their regular break-ups, Peter would be there with a box of tissues and a shoulder to cry on.

Peter himself was in a long-term relationship in Shropshire with a girl named Jo. They often made up a foursome in outings with Gary and Siobhán. Almost inevitably, both relationships came to an end and when they did Peter had a succession of what

Siobhán described as unsuitable and unstable girlfriends. He was inclined to agree with her.

Meanwhile, in America, Siobhán met, dated and received proposals of marriage from several high-flying career academics. Peter sensed that his unrequited love for her was destined to stay that way. 'Although I had not yet made her aware of my intentions,' he says, 'I knew that I had to take affirmative action before it was too late – though I had no real reason to believe she would be interested in a serious relationship. I didn't really feel worthy of her.'

However, one strange prediction gave him hope. He had a tarot reading from a girl at the public relations firm where he worked. In the course of the reading she identified a 'Dark Princess' who held the key to his future happiness. Peter had no doubt of the identity of the dark, feminine presence revealed in the cards.

Guided by the tarot, Peter was advised to pursue this challenge – but was warned that the 'Dark Princess' wanted a long-term, committed relation-ship. Anything less than total dedication to a joint union would be destined to failure. Peter accepted his mission and set off for America to conquer his princess.

Self-consciously, Peter admits he always felt it was amazing good fortune on his part that Siobhán fell in love with him and agreed to become his wife and mother to his children. 'Even now I have to pinch myself to believe it,' he says. 'I always felt there had been some administrative error in the great celestial relationship record book which teamed her with me.'

For her part, Siobhán did not make it easy for her eager suitor.

Peter advances the theory that she deliberately misunderstood his intentions because she was protecting herself from future hurt and did not believe him capable of maintaining a mature and enduring relationship.

'I had treated my long-term girlfriend Jo and a string of other women pretty shabbily,' Peter admits. 'Siobhán would make transatlantic phone calls, usually early in the morning, to berate me and urge me to change my ways. Somehow the fact she showed such interest convinced me that she must see some potential in me.'

Moving out of the house they shared in Telford, Peter and Jo split the proceeds of the sale of the house they had bought jointly. Peter, determined to make a fresh start, resigned from his job and packed his bags for America. 'The official plan was for me to travel around America, but in reality I had made up my mind to try to persuade Siobhán to marry me,' he says.

Siobhán invited him to stay at her New York apartment and the two spent quality time together socialising and getting to know each other away from the pressures of past relationships. Siobhán delighted in the fact that Peter proposed to her on the second date. While admitting it was probably true, Peter says it actually took him much longer to pluck up the courage – and risk what he felt was inevitable rejection.

However, he did buy an engagement ring – of sorts. He had been hanging around Siobhán's apartment for weeks, while she gently hinted that it was time for him to move on and take to the road. Eventually she agreed to accompany him on the first stage of a planned trip to the Deep South. Peter, a skilled guitarist, had been anxious to make a musical pilgrimage, visiting the legendary home of country and western music, the blues and rock 'n' roll. 'Siobhán and I had taken a fantastic, adventure-filled road trip from New York to Tennessee,' he says excitedly. 'She then flew back to her teaching post at Columbia and I went on to New Orleans.'

During an extended stay in New Orleans he secretly bought a ring and determined to propose. 'The ring was a pink tanzanite in a delicate, filigree setting. It wasn't expensive but given my state of penury at that time, having been in America for almost six months and unable to work because of visa restrictions, it was a genuine and heartfelt gesture.'

Peter had moved back into Siobhán's apartment and now was seriously in danger of outstaying his welcome. She urged him to hit the road again and explore other areas of America before his visa expired and he was legally bound to leave the country and return to England.

'It was kind of embarrassing,' he says, laughing at the absurdity of it all. 'I wanted to marry her and she kept urging me to be on my way. Finally I knew I could put it off no longer, and put my master plan in place.'

He took her to the cinema to see *Sea of Love*, starring Al Pacino and Ellen Barkin, and on to what he thought would be a romantic dinner in a restaurant in a New York restaurant featured in the film. However, events did not turn out as planned. The restaurant, an Italian eatery, looked nothing like it had on screen.

'The romantic setting I envisaged,' he says ruefully, 'was in fact a film set. In reality the restaurant was mediocre. I almost abandoned my grand plan. I had wanted something special and memorable – not memorable for being such a letdown.'

Brushing aside his disappointment, Peter decided to seize the moment anyway. As he tells the story, it sounds like Woody Allen trying to woo an elusive Diane Keaton: he full of doubts and angst; she confident, assured and faintly amused by his discomfiture.

As if in slow motion Peter can still recall the proposal frame by frame. 'In my head I was down on one knee, proffering the open jewel box with the glittering betrothal ring and saying, "Will you marry me?"

'Cut to Siobhán. *Eyes sparkling, dazzled by the ring, thrilled by the longed-for proposal.* Rewind... It did not quite play out that way,' admits Peter wryly. 'What really happened was that I pulled the ring out of my pocket with no preamble, thrust it at her and said, "I thought you might like this ring."'

Siobhán wasn't going to make it easy for Peter. Instead, without ceremony, she took the ring and hesitated before expressing an opinion. 'Yes,' she said cautiously, 'I like it.' Peter agonised as she toyed with the ring, seemingly contemplating whether to put it on the third finger of her left hand. He held his breath as she slipped the ring on to her engagement finger. Then she changed her mind and moved it to the other hand. Satisfied that it fitted the right hand, Siobhán carried on eating as if nothing had happened.

Peter never did pluck up courage to ask his Dark

Princess to marry him. Gradually, though, as he prepared to return to England, an understanding was reached that he would go back and look for a house for them to move into together.

Siobhán was increasingly homesick and the failing health of her ageing parents worried her. She was ready to return home, take up a post at a British university and settle down with Peter.

The two married in the Roman Catholic Cathedral in Shrewsbury on 29 August 1992.

Siobhán was a radiant bride in a glamorous floor-length wedding gown with a Renaissance-style gold skirt and embroidered ivory bodice.

Surrounded by family and friends, the couple took their wedding vows and faced the future with the traditional unspoken wish that they would live happily ever after.

Chapter Four

With Dignity and Courage

Early in 2007 the cancer returned. Siobhán travelled several times between Belfast and the Royal Marsden Hospital in London. Eventually her health deteriorated to the point where doctors insisted she was no longer fit to fly. Her treatment was transferred to Belfast City Hospital and her day-to-day care taken over by a local GP, Dr Susan McGarrity.

'The notes and letter I received from the Marsden,' says Dr McGarrity, 'made it pretty plain that Siobhán's disease was now terminal. There was really nothing more they could do for her. She had been apprised of the situation.

'The Marsden proposed a series of treatment which would include radiotherapy and chemotherapy, but those would not halt the disease – only keep her comfortable.'

Siobhán had been warned that the disease was likely to spread to her brain and a course of radiotherapy was planned to slow down its progress. She did not live long enough to have this treatment, and thank God her mental faculties were not unduly affected.

Dr McGarrity remembers clearly the first time she went to visit Siobhán at her home in south Belfast. 'Knowing the seriousness of her illness and the late stage she had entered, I was surprised to find her up and about. The family had just acquired a new Labrador puppy, Ruby, and I was amazed that Siobhán was capable of controlling her.'

The melanoma Siobhán had suffered seven years previously had returned and, despite radical breast surgery, the cancer had now spread to her lungs.

'Reading the notes, it was apparent that the disease had taken the same course as previously, first melanoma and then attacking the lungs,' explains Dr McGarrity.

'The medical notes from the Marsden did state that there had been a query over the progress of the disease seven years before. Seems that it had regressed of its own accord – there was no mention in the notes of any possible interventions – divine or otherwise.'

Dr McGarrity describes Siobhán as a most unusual woman. 'She really was a special kind of person. Certainly I wasn't used to meeting anyone quite so articulate. On one occasion she talked to me about her disease. She painted a graphic picture.'

Siobhán told the doctor, 'I feel like my body is an apple and every day there are more and more black spots and bruising. Soon my whole body will be covered.'

Being almost the same age as Siobhán and a mother herself, Dr McGarrity admits that she held a particular affection for her. There was also a more personal reason: the doctor's own husband had also been diagnosed with cancer. He and Siobhán were undergoing treatment at the same time. Dr McGarrity, while discussing Siobhán, revealed that he was 'very poorly'.

'Siobhán's disease had gathered momentum,' she says, 'and as she got more sick, she seemed to gain more strength. Her strength of character and resilience meant that she remained positive up to the end – though she did know she was dying.

'She had an acceptance of that fact and never shied away from discussing what would happen to the family after she had gone. Her concerns were always for the husband Peter and the children, Oscar and Constance.

'Her attitude was impressive,' says the doctor, who all too often these days is confronted with patients losing their battle against cancer. She offers this insight, 'I honestly don't believe Siobhán was afraid of dying. She was a girl of remarkable faith. She accepted her fate and in our discussions no avenues were closed.

'She was intelligent and open; she heard what was said about the upcoming stages of the disease. The Marsden had suggested she might have between nine and eighteen months. Siobhán never asked me to be more specific. In the event she lived for just another four months.'

Siobhán was admitted to Belfast City Hospital's Cancer Centre in Holy Week 2007.

'We took her in for some pain management and specialist nursing,' Dr McGarrity explains. 'It was expected that she would return home and the plan would have been to arrange hospice care as she got nearer the end. The end came suddenly, but I know Siobhán died with great dignity and courage.'

Nurses on the ward at the Cancer Centre, trained to deal with dying patients, were also struck by Siobhán's level of acceptance.

On the day she died, at noon on Easter Saturday, 7 April, one of the nurses put her thoughts into words. 'Siobhán slipped away peacefully into the arms of God – he refused to let her suffer any longer.'

Now that we have traced the course of Siobhán's final years through the memories of those close to her, let us look at her experience as she recounts it in her own words. Each of the remaining chapters closes with an extract from Siobhán's Story.

SIOBHÁN'S STORY: WE'LL MEET AGAIN

On 5 May 1999 I closed and locked the door of my office in the Literature Department of the University of Sussex, nestling beneath the hills of the South Downs.

The day was warm and sunny as I set off across campus to walk the five miles to Brighton railway station by way of the seafront. It was 1991 and I'd taken up the post of lecturer at this most modern and radical of universities after eight years in America as student and then teacher.

My head was filled with observations on the work of students already seen that day and I made a mental note of work to be discussed with those pupils whose tutorials I had hastily rearranged.

Mentally I also ran through the research needed for an upcoming guest lecture and wondered if I'd left behind any important papers or reference books in my rush to leave the building.

Certainly I'd left my outdoor coat and a small

overnight bag, deciding that I already had more than enough to carry. My briefcase was, as usual, filled to bursting with paperwork, publications and unmarked essays.

There was no way of knowing that more than a year later I would still not have returned to my paper-strewn desk in that office with its sign on the door 'Professor Siobhán Kilfeather, Lecturer, English Literature'.

Sitting on the train from Paddington to Shrewsbury on the way home to our cottage in Shropshire, some 220 miles from Brighton, I replayed in my head the previous evening's telephone conversation with my husband Peter. He was at home with our two children, Constance, who was four, and Oscar, who was coming up to two. I had carefully timed my phone call till after the children were in bed and the Manchester United game against Liverpool had finished on Match of the Day.

Peter was depressed. He couldn't disguise it, though he was making a real effort to sound normal. At the time I thought, 'If this is how he reacts to a disappointing football score, what will he feel like if the results of my tests are positive? He's getting things a bit out of proportion.' But in my heart of hearts I knew the reason.

'Why won't you tell me what's wrong?' I asked yet again. The only explanation I could force out of him

just didn't ring true. He tried to make me believe that his upset was because Paul Ince had scored an equaliser against Manchester United in a 2–2 draw. But I knew my husband too well. The unspoken message in his voice was stirring up in me a feeling of impending doom.

'Expect me home tomorrow,' I said quickly. Already I was visualising changes I would need to make in my schedule. Peter wouldn't admit it but I knew instinctively that he had received the results of a biopsy I had undergone a month earlier at a local hospital at Stoke.

His voice told me what he refused to put into words. The test was positive. I had cancer.

All the way home my mind refused to let go of the word 'cancer'. I tried to escape into the make-believe world of books – always my escape from the real world – but my mind refused to concentrate.

The motion of the train seemed to echo my thoughts: Living with cancer, dying from cancer, living with cancer, dying from cancer...

It was close to midnight before I drove down the dark and narrow lane to our home, a mile above a cross-country road outside Shrewsbury.

Peter's face was etched with pain and worry, but still he tried to distract me from hearing the bad news. He claimed tiredness – trying to put off for just one more day the stark fact that we were staring into the unknown. Our lives were about to change irrevocably.

'Let's deal with it in the morning,' he said.

However, I was not to be put off – the suspense was agonising.

Knowing that I would be difficult to contact during classes at the university, I had instructed the hospital to leave a message on the answering machine.

'Let me hear the message, right now,' I demanded.

But Peter had already wiped the tape clean. As if by erasing the message he could erase the truth.

Finally, close to tears and as the clock struck midnight, he gave me the bad news: 'The results are positive. You have to go straight away and see Dr Edmunds at North Staffordshire Hospital. Tomorrow.'

Climbing the stairs to bed, I looked in on our two children, sleeping peacefully. They could not know that their mother's life, and inevitably theirs too, was about to spin out of all our control. We could not begin to fathom what would happen next.

That night in bed I clung to Peter, who lay rigid with fear beside me. Each time I tried to close my eyes I was tormented with feelings of stark terror.

Neither of us slept a wink all night.

Still the refrain in my head: Living with cancer, dying from cancer, living with cancer, dying from cancer.

My body had been invaded – I had cancer.

The nightmare had started back in 1997 when I was pregnant with my second baby. I went to my GP in Shropshire and told him that I had a mole on my back that worried me. I thought it might be cancerous. I'd read the leaflets in the surgery and it seemed to me that I had the symptoms of malignant melanoma.

He said, 'No, no, no, it's only a mole. You've been reading too many women's magazines.'

All the same, it was bothering me, I said, and suggested I should arrange to have it removed privately, but he said he would refer me to a local hospital in Stoke to have it removed on the NHS.

I was still waiting eighteen months later and when I went back to the surgery to check whether the referral had gone through, another doctor looked at my records on the computer and told me to go straight to hospital that day.

It was as if someone had punched me in the stomach. There was no delay this time and I knew then it must be pretty serious and could be skin cancer.

The biopsy was performed at Shrewsbury Hospital and the surgeon told me there was a fifty–fifty chance that it was malignant. That was the first real indication of a major crisis. The word 'malignant' was used rather than 'cancer'.

After the hospital appointment I made my way to my husband's office in Shrewsbury and he took me to lunch at the local fish and chip shop. Not surprisingly perhaps, my usual healthy appetite had deserted me and I couldn't eat a thing. Peter was worried, though it didn't stop him clearing his plate. Over our meal I told him that I thought the growth was malignant.

Knowing that doctors are not in the business of scaring you, I thought if he said fifty–fifty there was a good chance it was actually ninety–ten.

That was in late April 1999, just before the May bank holiday, and the four of us had rented the village hall where we had held Constance's birthday party a few weeks before. We had taken it over again to bounce around on the trampoline and play with toys that were too big to be used in our house because work was going on building an extension and conservatory.

The test results would probably come at the end of that weekend and I thought, 'What if this is the last carefree weekend of my entire life?'

My mind was filled with thoughts of how much I loved Peter and how lucky I was to have the children. I worried for all of them and wondered what it would mean to their lives if the mole had become malignant.

One of the worst times was when a dermatologist came to see me in my home. He told me the depth of the disease and said it was the worst case of malignant melanoma he had ever seen.

I put it to him straight: 'Am I going to die?'

His answer was to ask: 'Are you a religious person?'

I was so shocked that I just fainted away. I was standing up and he had to pick me up off the floor.

I finally managed: 'If I'm going to die, how long do you think I've got?' He turned his face away from me and didn't answer.

My mind went into overdrive after he'd gone. If I've got three or four months, I should try and finish my contribution to The Field Day Anthology of Irish Writing, a monumental work I'd been involved with for several years.

My head is so full of clutter I can't think straight. I should write to old friends I've lost touch with. Tell them I'm going to die.

I can't seem to get things into proportion. The most important considerations are obviously my children and my husband, but also my work is important to me. My writing, my book, my students.

Should I spend the last twelve hours of my life reading Jane Austen or writing an essay or singing nursery rhymes to my children?

The first operation was in North Staffordshire Hospital in Stoke. The surgeon had made one wide incision on my back, taking off a wide deep area of skin about six inches square where the original melanoma had struck. Some weeks later, another wide incision, though on a smaller area of my knee for a suspected melanoma which turned out to be non-malignant.

In the same hospital I underwent reconstructive surgery. They removed a large area of skin from my thigh and grafted it on to my back. This operation was not a success. Would they do it again?

At that time the next treatment was scheduled to be a course of chemotherapy along with Interferon and possibly an experimental drug treatment.

In January 2000 I reported to the Royal Marsden Hospital in London for post-operative treatment after my surgery in Stoke. I was confident I would be given the all-clear – the cancer seemed to be in remission and I'd never felt better.

Instead they dropped a bombshell – I now had secondary cancer and it had already spread to my lungs. I was in a state of shock.

Somehow a strange feeling of invincibility had convinced me that I would never have to face such devastating news. Now I replayed the conversation and the words the doctor had used again and again in my head: 'Secondaries – lung cancer – very serious.'

They told me that chemotherapy was the only course of action. I would have to undergo a particularly aggressive treatment – they admitted they wouldn't have tried the procedure on anyone who wasn't young and fit. I didn't know whether to laugh or cry.

For most of the past year I had been taking part in clinical trials for a new form of non-invasive treatment based on a combination of drugs. Now I would need four weeks to allow these chemicals to be flushed from my system before the chemotherapy could be started.

I went home and began to put my affairs in order. There was a lot to be organised regarding the children, Oscar's nursery and Constance's school, as well as arrangements for someone to look after them while I was in hospital. Initially it was to be a period of five to seven days in hospital undergoing the chemotherapy and then two or three weeks at home before a second and possibly a third stay as an in-patient.

A review would be made after the second course of treatment around the end of March. If the results were not encouraging, it might be decided not to proceed with a third round of chemotherapy. At that stage no one could say what the effects or the results would be – but they were willing to try.

No one was quoting odds on the treatment

working but I was reassured even by the fact that they were prepared to give me it at all.

As part of my regular on-going treatment to relieve stress, once a week I went for a massage. I had not been able to lie comfortably on my back because I got that sensation of panicking and not being able to breathe. These may have been normal symptoms of lung cancer but they might just as easily have been caused by hypertension and anxiety.

For a couple of months now I had also suffered from back pain. I also had to contend with pains around the groin and the abdomen. I wouldn't be surprised if those were areas where I did now have cancer, though of course they could be anxiety-related.

Some of these symptoms I described to a wonderful South African doctor at North Staffordshire Hospital, Mr Prinsloo, together with a catalogue of other totally unrelated symptoms. I went in to see him some months previously complaining of earache, which I thought was a symptom of a brain tumour. He quickly disabused me of that idea. 'Earache is not a symptom of brain tumour,' he told me. 'I've no intention of telling you what is because you'll start to develop those symptoms.'

There was also the time when I rang the cancer

clinic at the Royal Marsden complaining of blood in my stools. It turned out to be an excess of beetroot juice, which I had been drinking as part of my healthy high-vegetable diet.

On another occasion Mr Prinsloo told me that he thought the melanoma on my knee was cancerous and he had decided to send a sample to the laboratory for testing. I told him I knew it was cancerous because I could feel the cancer coursing through my veins. 'What you're feeling coursing through your veins is adrenalin,' he assured me. 'You don't feel cancer coursing through your veins.'

It's very difficult to talk about symptoms at this stage because every ache and pain felt like cancer to me. It would not be an exaggeration to say that the past year had been like a waking nightmare.

Night-time was worst. I lay awake in a cold sweat clinging to Peter. The fear of dying made me feel desperate and almost demented. The way I have survived this phase is chiefly with the help of antidepressants.

But you can't go on like that for ever and with the passage of time I needed to refocus. This was possible largely through the advice and help of Mr Prinsloo. He put it on the line: 'None of us know when we are going to die. Think about what you are going to do with your living. You could walk out of this hospital today and be run over by a bus. Try not to let the fear of death overcome what it is you want to do with the rest of your life.'

Chapter Five

She Always Laughed

Oscar Jameson knows what he misses most about his mummy. 'I miss making her laugh,' he says poignantly. 'I always tried my jokes out on her and she always laughed.'

Even though he is only ten, Oscar knows what he wants to do when he grows up. 'A stand-up comedian,' he says without hesitation. This may come a surprise to people who know Oscar as he seems a shy young boy. 'Around grown-ups I often don't know what to say,' he admits, 'but with my friends I'm always talking and joking. It's my favourite thing, making people laugh. Even some of the teachers have seen my stand-up comedy routine and they think it's very funny.'

Oscar is happily settled in an excellent school in

Belfast, to where the family moved three years before Siobhán's illness returned. He is an able and well-liked pupil.

Warming to the theme of his future career, Oscar springs another surprise. 'I model myself on Billy Connolly,' he says. 'I watch his videos and even steal some of his jokes, though I really prefer writing my own material.'

Oscar is proud that many people say he is like his mother. 'We share lots of attitudes,' he says, 'especially about people. We never like anyone who thinks they are better than others – especially if it's because they just have more money.'

In a memorial book at Siobhán's funeral, Oscar wrote this tribute to his mother: 'Mummy was nice because she always let everyone's opion [*sic*] count. Oscar.'

'There was one special way we were like each other,' he says thoughtfully. A pause. 'It's an S word – its not "sympathetic" – it's more like we understand people. Oh, I know, the word is "sensitive". Mummy and I are sensitive.'

Apart from enjoying making her laugh, Oscar shared another great passion with his mother: football. The whole family would gather around the television to cheer their favourite teams, Manchester United – and Ireland.

'We liked to watch and work out what the players were going to do,' explains Oscar. 'I think it's an A word – something like "analyse".'

Oscar is an enthusiastic player himself and the word is that he is very good. Asked if he would like to be a professional footballer, he answers with surprising maturity. 'Sure, but so would most of the other boys – and some of the girls. You've got to be really, really good to be a professional. You need years of training and hard work – but that's not to say I won't try my best.'

People tend to fall in love with this tall, handsome, fair-haired boy – just like they did with his mother – but, like her, he is discriminating in his tastes. 'Just because someone likes me doesn't mean I like them,' he says matter-of-factly. 'I like to watch how people behave and then decide if I want them to be my friend... My mum was the same. We would never be friends with someone who was unkind to other people.'

A member of the school council, Oscar is passionately against bullying. 'We did have a boy in my school who was bullying some of the younger kids,' he says. 'He was the same age as me, but I'm a lot taller than him. One day in the playground I went up and told him that what he was doing was wrong. He said he would stop. I hope he does because we have to protect the younger ones. My mum taught me that.'

Oscar is certainly his mother's son. Any parent would be proud to have him as a son. 'I can still hear her voice in my head,' he says, 'and I talk to her – I think she's gone to heaven.'

Constance Gilfedder, to whom Siobhán restored the Irish form of her own surname, would like her mum remembered by the kind of story she used to tell 'when I was little'. Like the story of mischievous Suki:

'Suki is a spider with six legs who lives in our back yard. He is married to a thrush called Amarylla. They have eight children: four thrush-sized spiders and four spider-sized thrushes. Suki likes going to different places by hiding on the roof of the car. He went to the beach, to the park, to school and lots of other places. Once, he went to the zoo and accidentally got lost. He ended up in a lion's cage, where the lion tried to eat him. But before he could, it got a thorn stuck in its paw, so Suki pulled it out and in return the lion didn't eat him. Then a little girl accidentally dropped an ice cream on him and he froze solid. Eventually a stray dog found him and licked him until he thawed out enough to move. Then the dog said its name was Jack, and Suki climbed on his back. Jack took Suki back to the car park, where he climbed on the roof of the car just in time and went home.'

SIOBHÁN'S STORY: ME AND MY CHILDREN

Mostly these days I like to write for my children. Constance won't forget even if the stories I've made up for them over the years are never published. The characters we have made up will continue to influence their lives.

We have these two characters, Rosamond Almond and Suki Spider, who are part of our family mythology and I'm sure Peter and Constance will keep them alive for Oscar. Every family has these stories and just because they are not published does not diminish their importance – a story is important even if it is only one person who hears it.

Constance and I have learned a lot about each other through sharing our imagination and making things up together and mythologising our lives. We make up stories about the dogs, the house, the garden, family holidays, all the ordinary everyday things of our lives together.

We've also talked about my illness and the possibility that I might die. We told her about the things that were happening.

There were so many people visiting and phoning up. Rather than let Constance make something up, perhaps even worse than the reality, I talked to her and said that I might die. I told her that people who have cancer sometimes do die, but that even death is not the end of life. Like her grandmother, who died in 1998, she still will be able to talk to me when I'm up in heaven and visit my grave.

There is only one area in which I haven't been honest. I have pretended to her that I'm not frightened of dying. She is not frightened of dying – she believes it is something we all welcome and embrace.

My mother lived with us for eighteen months before she died. Constance understands that now nanny is in heaven she doesn't come back to visit and we can't pop up to visit her, though we do go and put flowers on her grave and talk to her then.

Mum has been gone long enough now for Constance to be aware that death does indeed represent a kind of loss. And I think she expresses that most often by saying that if I die she wants to go with me – she doesn't want to stay behind. I don't know how she will cope if my illness gets worse.

She's a sweet, caring child, a very good child. Not a day passes when she doesn't say, 'Let me kiss your scars, Mummy. Let me see if I can make it better.' She arranges cushions for me and tells Oscar, 'Don't jump on Mummy, her back hurts.' She is considerate to her father, Peter, and gives him extra time to get on with all the things he has to do while I am ill.

The hardest thing I find is when she's showing a

different side of her childish personality and being difficult and crying and whingeing. I have to make a conscious effort not to pull the sickness card and say, 'Let Mummy rest.' I endeavour not to take advantage of her sweet nature.

Oscar, I think, suffers a lot when I'm absent. He seems to know intuitively that I'm not well. He's a sunny little boy and I can't imagine how his little mind will adjust if one day he does not see me again. He's very attached to his father and very attached to Constance. Though I know he will never be able to get over the death of his mother, in a way he will come to terms with it.

One of the reasons for choosing his guardians, Liane Jones and Jamie Buxton, is because Jamie lost both his parents in childhood and he will understand some of the issues that Oscar will need to face and hopefully be able to help him. At least he will have some experience to share with him that other people may not have been able to express.

We have also done some things in case I die that I never thought we would – like having a family portrait taken at Christmas in the studio. My parents and grandparents always had family portraits done in a studio.

I've also been trying to record, with varying degrees of success, a tape of me reading the two children a bedtime story so that they could listen to my voice, though I did say to Peter it could be more upsetting than comforting. He would have to be the judge of that should the time come when I'm not here.

The way I discipline the children has been governed by the uncertainty of my illness. Both Peter and I try not to reprimand them in any way that makes them feel they are not living up to our expectations of them.

We try to spell out how much we care for them and leave them with lots of positive affirmations of praise so that, should they lose me, then hopefully they will not be left with the thought that it's some kind of punishment.

They are very happy children. Any difficulties or uncertainties they may have in their world are concerned with the environment outside the home, at school or with friends, not with any doubts about whether their parents love them.

Chapter Six

In the Name of Art

Siobhán Kilfeather was an internationally acclaimed authority on Irish writing and feminism. She graduated in English Literature from Cambridge, was awarded her doctorate at Princeton University and held faculty posts at Columbia University, the University of Sussex and Queen's University, Belfast.

Much of her work is academic in nature and so is generally considered accessible and pertinent only to her peers and students.

Wearing her professorial hat, she delighted in educating, entertaining and enlightening her readers and students. One speciality was introducing the rich oral tradition of Ireland with its stories, recitations, music and performance. Hers was a colourful world of historians, genealogists, storytellers and entertainers, skilfully interwoven with history, tradition and politics.

She herself celebrated the 'wild Irish' of history typified by women displaying their femininity through flowing clothing and tumbling locks of hair. She evoked the Goddess of Memory, Mnemosyne, and delighted in expressing the opinion: 'Every view of things that is not wonderful is false.'

Siobhán's masterwork, which she thought would be left unfinished when she had her first brush with death, was a collaboration with other female academics. She was a contributing editor of *The Field Day Anthology of Irish Writing*, working with other academics on *Volumes IV and V: Irish Women's Writing and Traditions*. These volumes are now considered the definitive work on Irish women's writing.

Siobhán and her fellow editors were honoured at two receptions to introduce their book to the literary world. A Dublin reception was attended by Ireland's first female president, Mary Robinson, and the scholars were also honoured at a champagne reception in the Irish Embassy in London on International Women's Day 2003.

Siobhán took wicked delight in telling people that she had edited the chapters on sexuality. 'It isn't as racy as it sounds,' she was to admit, 'but it always got everyone's attention.' The section 'Sexuality (1685–2001)' covered stories of seduction, prostitution, pregnancy, and childbirth and child murder. Siobhán brought her powerful gifts of research and knowledge of Irish literature, ancient and modern, to recount fascinating stories of seduction, abductions, transvestites, irregular priests and hoary old lechers.

A particular favourite subject of hers was covered in 'Romanticism (1801–1917)', which introduced the readers to a cluster of new ideas and practices such as described in 'The Life and Transactions of a Female Prostitute' and 'The Ballad of the Wandering Girl'. Sounding at once charmed and outraged, Siobhán presented these stories as absolute weepies, tales of innocence seduced and betrayed.

The PhD thesis that Siobhán completed at Princeton was never formally published because she felt it was unfinished and would benefit from more work. One of her colleagues, Dr Jayne Lewis, Professor of English at the University of Southern California, explained, 'It is groundbreaking and needs to be made available, but Siobhán was a perfectionist and believed she could make it even better. She ran out of time.'

The thesis, bound in two volumes and last updated in 1989, was on eighteenth-century Irish women's writing. The introduction draws attention to the main themes of the work: 'Seventeenth- and eighteenth-century writing might be said to organise sexuality into two broad categories – approved and unapproved modes of sexual expression. The line between the legal and illegal.' Siobhán goes on to quote a piece of Irish folklore: 'It is a good family that has neither whore nor rogue in it.'

She concludes: 'Representations of sexuality seem polarised between versions of authentic Ireland, a realm of purity, and versions which insist that the true Irish character is ribald and promiscuous.'

Her contribution to *The Field Day Anthology* also uncovers writings about the white-slave trade and the missing-child syndrome. 'In Ireland the empty crib and the missing child is a powerful symbol of a State that has abused rather than cherished the children it is constitutionally bound to nurture.'

She sees a distinctly non-feminist viewpoint in the practice of women suing men for 'Breach of Promise of Marriage'. In one case in a nineteenth-century Dublin court the plaintiff demanded two thousand punts (Irish pounds). The case having been proved, she received half that amount, plus sixpence costs.

Siobhán's discussions of sexuality also deal with the inevitable results of 'Pregnancy, Childbirth and the Consequences of Child Bearing (1768–1849)'. In a ballad entitled 'No More Come to Woo' a young maiden's lament tells the all too familiar tale of being left holding the baby:

I was simple I own,
And should better have known
Than to trust such deceivers as you,

He that won't, when he may,
When he will shall have nay,
Then pray you no more
Come to Woo.

Siobhán also found early examples of the ever-popular modern advice columns in women's magazines and publications. In the nineteenth century these were usually copied from conduct books. One such column, in the Londonderry *Sentinel & North West Advertiser* (1833), offered maxims for the married. Under the heading 'Codes of Instructions for Gentlemen' it gave advice such as: 'Be strictly moral in your conduct – consider what you would think if your wife should become immoral in her conduct.'

Women were presented with a much longer list of instructions:

'Never take upon yourself to censor your husband's words and do not read lectures to him.

'Command attention by always being attentive to him.

'Appear always flattered by the little he does for you, which will excite him to perform more.

'As men are vain, never wound his vanity.

'A wife may have more sense than her husband, but she should never seem to know it.

'Seem always to obtain information from him, especially before company, though you may pass yourself for a simpleton.

'Never forget that a wife owes all her importance to her husband.'

We can only imagine the mutterings of outrageous indignation that would have been coming from Siobhán as she read and passed on these anti-feminist words.

Coming from a family in which her father was a Catholic and her mother born a Protestant, Siobhán took some time in the anthology to explore the problems of mixed marriages. From the mid-nineteenth century, it seems, mixed marriage developed as a site of domestic conflict.

Siobhán also produced several narratives exploring the troubling universal themes of domestic violence, jealousy, manipulation, infanticide and conflict over child custody.

Citing several reports from 1867, she drew

attention to the enduring practice of newspapers to report sex scandals, murder, insanity and exploitation, particularly of the poor.

Quoting the *Pall Mall Gazette* of 1867, she attached great importance to a feature entitled 'A Night on the Casual Ward' which reported the miserable lives of prostitutes living near army camps at the Curragh outside Dublin.

A related article dealt with the Contagious Disease Act (1881), revealing that senior officials in the British Army were concerned about the spread of venereal disease. Also included were articles on 'Childbirth (1742–1955)' and 'The Work of the Midwife (1932)'.

Siobhán never flinched from getting down and dirty and exploring the crudest of sexual practices and their consequences. She also responded to love stories told in the ancient Irish legends which touched on mystical charms and superstitions. Her exposure of 'Popular Superstitions and Folklore' included the dire warning: 'Hatred and revenge are as potent as love in the construction of desire.'

She sited Salome as the figure who, in the literature, visual arts and theatrical arts of the late nineteenth century, represented aggressive feminism and the persuasive aesthetic of the decadents.

Outside her usual area of study on women,

sexuality and feminism, Siobhán was fascinated by the universal power inherent in one particular Irish relic. The skull of Oliver Plunkett (1625–81) is exhibited in St Peter's Church, Drogheda. This grisly relic of the Irish martyr expressed the double-edged themes of the sacred and the profane and the deepest mysteries of life and death, Siobhán wrote. So Plunkett lives on through the enduring fascination and visible presence of his head.

Siobhán herself lives on through her education, erudition and wonderful ability to see both the sublime and the ridiculous. A perfect example of her unique perception of art and culture can be seen in her portrait of a great city that was close to her heart. The following extract from her *Dublin: A Cultural and Literary History* appears by kind permission of Signal Books, Oxford:

Homage to Dublin

The seeds of my romance with Dublin were sown long before I was born. In the late 1940s my mother, a working-class Ulster Protestant girl, moved to Dublin for a year. It was probably the biggest adventure of her life before marriage and she was lucky to be befriended independently by two of the most interesting writers living in the city at that time. The poet and novelist Patrick Kavanagh lived in a cold, bare flat on the Pembroke Road. My mother wrote him a fan letter. The first time he took her out to lunch he had to hunt through pockets and under chairs for enough coins to buy two bowls of soup and a pot of tea. She met Seosamh Mac Grianna's partner, Peggy, in a bakery. They became friends and eventually Peggy took her to meet the writer, who was living separately from his partner and son because of the social stigma attached to unmarried couples. Mac Grianna was an Irish language writer who depended on translation work and on the socially conservative world of Irish language publishing, where he believed that the influence of the Catholic Church put him under threat. He was also struggling in terrible poverty and under that pressure had begun to show symptoms of the mental illness that enveloped the second half of his life. Perhaps if they had been wealthier and more successful, Kavanagh and Mac Grianna would have had less time for a girl who had left school at fourteen and spent most of her life working as a shop assistant. But my mother was also intelligent, very well-read, and innocently enthusiastic about everything to do with literature.

My mother came back to Belfast, became a Catholic as much through political as religious conversion, married my father, and spent most of my childhood talking about how much happier we would be if we could afford to escape the brutal philistinism (as she saw it) of Belfast, move to Dublin and live the life of the mind. A trip to Dublin was our favourite day out. We did not have a car, so we would take the Enterprise train from Belfast to Connolly Station, determinedly love the bad coffee and biscuits, and be thrilled when we crossed the border and the money changed. If I were pressed I would have to concede that Connolly is one of the ugliest railway stations in the world but my heart lifts whenever I arrive there, and descend the steps to Amiens Street. I cannot really remember all that we did on those days out or why we enjoyed them so much.

My mother, who had been a child evacuated to the countryside during the war, associated Dublin with good food (!) and she always bought sausages, tea and cakes to take home with us. We walked about the main shopping thoroughfares and had picnics in St Stephen's Green. We went to galleries and bookshops and always visited at least two pubs to soak up the atmosphere. I remember the deep contentment that came over my father one lunchtime because Sean O'Faolain, a writer he admired, was having a drink in the same pub. He did not want to speak to O'Faolain, just to breathe the same atmosphere. In the 1970s Dublin seemed a very shabby city, but it inspired passion, and of course it was liberating to escape the horrors of Belfast even for a day.

Twice I might have gone to university in Dublin, but both times I swerved at the last moment to go further afield, reckoning that I was bound to live in Dublin some day. It has not happened yet, but I am not altogether sorry that the city still retains for me the thrill of a holiday destination, even when I am there, as I am most often these days, to work in the much loved National Library of Ireland.

In common with most capital cities, Dublin has its fair share of fine architecture, statues and monuments, museums, galleries, parks and public spaces... But my own attraction to Dublin has always been based on its historical and cultural associations. I love to walk around the city and whenever I see a plaque commemorating a great life or an historic event I always want to know much more about it.

This is a history of life in the city... accounts of insurrection, repression, strikes, terror, executions, escapes and revolution; and events from the lives of scientists, artists, writers, musicians and sports people. Many years ago a friend brought me from Dublin a poster showing portraits of great Irish writers, and I was enraged that there was not a single woman to be seen...

My epilogue is an abecedary, a collection of scraps that is only apparently arbitrary: a homage to my jazz-playing, football-loving, whisky-drinking, star-gazing Jewish husband, and to those days out in pubs, bookshops, galleries and teashops with mother and father...

As a visitor to Dublin over the years I owe a tremendous debt of gratitude to several hosts and guides. Most of my Dublin friends are blow-ins, seduced by the city and unable to leave. My husband, Peter Jameson, is always at my side, helping out and making me laugh.

I never visit Dublin without thinking of my father and mother, who loved it.

Siobhán was a regular visitor to the Dublin Writers' Museum in Parnell Square in Dublin. She extolled the virtues of its idiosyncratic collection 'representing milestones in the progress of Irish literature from *Gulliver's Travels* to *Dracula*, *The Importance of Being Earnest*, *Ulysses* and *Waiting for Godot*'.

However, her favourite exhibit was 'a pair of John F. Kennedy's boxer shorts, recently purchased by an Irish businessman and briefly on display in a Dublin shop window'. Gleefully, she wrote, 'I hope this is a permanent addition to the Writer's Museum.'

Siobhán's published works are:

The Field Day Anthology of Irish Writing: Volumes IV and V: Irish Women's Writing and Traditions, edited by Siobhán Kilfeather *et al.*, Cork University Press, 2002

Dublin – A Cultural and Literary History, Signal Books, Oxford, 2005.

'Alice Maher's Materials' in *The Field Day Review*, Issue 2, 2006, Keough Institute for Irish Studies, University of Notre Dame, Indiana, USA.

Ellen & Derek Jameson

SIOBHÁN'S STORY: STRENGTHENED
BY LOURDES

Once the cancer was diagnosed, the first thing I wanted to do was to make a pilgrimage. There was a time after I came out of hospital when I experienced sheer naked terror and a great yearning overcame me.

One was to go home to Ireland. I realised how much I wished I had lived in Ireland and that now I wanted to go home. The other was to make a pilgrimage. At first I thought of combining those two things and visiting a sacred place in Ireland but there were various family and practical reasons why I thought it wouldn't work.

I remembered Lourdes from childhood – and the idea of pilgrimage became more important than the actual place.

When I was in the Royal Marsden having post-operative treatment I had to face my own difficulties looking at those who were ill and deformed. There were also people in the hospital in Stoke who had had very radical surgery.

One man had his jawbone replaced with part of a bone from his leg and he used to come in and stand at the end of my bed to chat and show me his scars. I was revolted and wanted to hide from him. Doing everything to deter him, I would put on headphones, read a book, turn away, scowl – anything to prevent making me look at him.

I know I was wrong and should have been able to confront his disabilities and find compassion in my heart. Into my head kept coming images of Lourdes and a fear I'd had since childhood that if I went there the sick would repel me.

My own child, Constance, now four, was teaching me every day about compassion. Her willingness to look at and kiss my scars to try to make them better astonished me. I thought my scars were repulsive, but she would actually touch and kiss them.

I hoped that going to Lourdes would allow me to become more like a child. The reality was that the visit has been even more spiritually fulfilling than I ever thought possible.

The biggest lesson I've learned from going to Lourdes is that you don't have to force yourself to be compassionate. You find it quite naturally in your heart when you allow genuine feelings to flow. While I've been here, I've been given the grace to feel that compassion and embrace complete strangers with love.

I find confession embarrassing. I don't like talking about myself. This is a place that teaches you to put self in its proper perspective.

For the first twenty-four hours I was haunted by a childhood superstition that you should not ask for things for yourself in prayer. In consequence I said a lot of prayers for other people – I lit candles for my parents, my children and a sick child in our village, but I didn't dare ask for myself.

It felt like I was being tested, to see if I would ask for a cure and then they would say, 'How dare you ask for yourself when there are so many sick people here? Why should God cure you when so many people are so much worse off than you?'

In a way I tried to double-bluff God by pretending that I don't care about myself at all and that I'm full of sanctimonious interest in other people. One of the lessons I learned from the Stations of the Cross is that we are allowed to pray for ourselves and not to just pray that God forgives my sins rather than cures my sickness.

And I now believe that He is not repelled by my asking to be cured. Though I accept He might not find that the right thing for me, I have now had the humility to ask. I found that the hardest thing to do. Perhaps having climbed up a flight of marble steps on aching knees as a form of penance humbled me enough to ask God for what I'd really come for: a cure for my cancer.

However, if a cure is not forthcoming, at least I

have been given strength and a degree of acceptance. In some ways it feels that if I were blasted by lightning and died now, that would be the easy route.

I could easily die now, but I'm frightened by something St Bernadette said when the visions came to her all those years ago. She asked the Blessed Mother, 'Why do we have to suffer so much before we die?'

I think I'm reconciled to the idea of death, as much as I'll ever be to the thought of putting my children in the hands of God and knowing that they will be all right.

But I'm scared of pain. I'm frightened of bottling out and being someone who loses their nerve. As a little girl, I used to read about people like the wartime heroine Odette and think, 'How could their minds go on in the face of torture? Why did they not collapse and grovel and snivel?' I've a terror of becoming abject in the face of pain.

In hospital in Stoke I had one of the most terrifying experiences of my life. There was a woman who had done that. She lost her nerve. I don't know what stage of the illness she was at, but she was refusing treatment, refusing intravenous treatment, and she was in bed opposite me. Her name was Madeline. She would have been between thirty-five and sixty – so broken in body and spirit that you couldn't tell.

I thought she was about fifty or sixty because there was a man there about that age I took to be her husband, though he could have been her brother. He would sit for hours holding her hand. Her elderly mother also visited regularly.

Madeline lay in bed and howled like an animal in pain. Every twenty minutes or so she would start to yell and the nurses would come and try to comfort her. On the hour, the doctors would come round and, as I understand it, they were obliged to inform her of her right to refuse treatment.

However, they were trying to persuade her that she should have treatment and they would try to put drips in her arms, but she would just cry out in pain and despair. I never heard one articulate word from her – neither 'yes' nor 'no'. She would just howl. The sound haunts me still.

That woman was suffering beyond anything I'd ever known. I thought my mother had suffered when she was dying, though she rarely revealed just how desperate she must have felt. I now know how many acts of courage she endured just to hold herself together. The effort it must have taken just to appear normal and to get on with life. To say simply, 'Yes, I'll have a cup of tea.'

Madeline was the exception. She had gone beyond the social constraints of being polite and suffering in silence. Most people don't give in even when they are experiencing extreme pain – and extreme fear.

I have to believe that, when the time comes, if my mother could get through it and other people bear their suffering with fortitude, I will be granted the same kind of courage. But still I am haunted by the fact that I may fall apart and disintegrate to the point of howling with pain and fear.

Strange as it may seem here in Lourdes, I feel blessed to have cancer. I still feel a lucky person. I feel lucky to have cancer. I think it's a blessing. Otherwise I would never have known the depth of goodness of friends and family. God has given me blessings where I least expected them.

Also, I've been spared the pain. I thought the pain would be the most terrible thing to bear and I had been dreading it. When the pain came at the time of my operations, it seemed to wash over me. I wasn't overwhelmed. I was always preoccupied with other things and never faced more than I could cope with. Even through the surgery.

That's not to say there won't be pain later but I'll face that when the time comes.

Today I feel blessed. Lourdes has given me that.

I still feel that maybe in some ways it is easier to get something like this when you are younger. Because even if I don't survive, I feel that I have *more strength to face death than, say, in twenty or thirty years' time.*

I've lit a candle for my GP in Shropshire, because some of the thoughts I've had about him have not been charitable. Perhaps, if he had taken my fears about the mole more seriously, he could have started treatment that much sooner.

Chapter Seven

Strangers at Home

Siobhán Marie Kilfeather presented her dissertation '"Strangers at Home": Political Fictions by Women in Eighteenth-Century Ireland' to the Faculty of Princeton University in her candidacy for the Degree of Doctor of Philosophy in October 1989. It was recommended for acceptance by the Department of English.

The full text of the two volumes awaits publication by Princeton University Press. However, much of what she wrote back then holds a particular poignancy now that she is no longer with us. The work contains the following dedication: 'For my mother and father, Rachel Docherty Kilfeather and John B. Kilfeather.'

'Strangers at Home' examines a selection of writings primarily from eighteenth-century Ireland and discusses the relationship between gender and other political categories represented in the writings. A door is opened slightly and the driving force of her work and passion is illuminated through this glimpse into her pioneering work in the field of feminism and traditional women's writing.

At a personal level, Siobhán reveals her own homesickness by writing: 'Insofar as this dissertation is concerned with the desire of home, discomfort at home and the experience of exile, it narrates my own concern at leaving Ireland for universities in England and the United States.'

She evokes the words of Samuel Johnson, who recorded the opinion of a Scottish Highlander that no one willingly leaves their home country. Siobhán wrote:

'It would be intolerable to live and work in a foreign country without the most complete confidence in the affection and support of one's family back at home.

'This dedication acknowledges a debt that can never be repaid. The paradox in the phrase "Strangers at Home" is also, however, the paradox of colonial experience. The settlers are never completely at ease in their adopted country, never find it possible to make an uncomplicated self-identification as Irish.'

Siobhán was fiercely Irish, proudly Celtic and passionately feminist.

The need for the safety and security of her homeland ensured that, despite success in America, a career in Sussex and a country home in Shropshire, she longed for Belfast. By the time her cancer had returned at Christmas 2006, she had already moved her whole family back to the city she loved so much.

Going home to Belfast in the twenty-first century must have been an astonishing revelation to Siobhán. Certainly there had been no 'Terror Tourists' in the war-torn city where she was born. In fact tourism was almost unheard of in Northern Ireland during the Troubles. Those outsiders who did come were mostly journalists and television crews covering the battles that were spawned by and prolonged the sectarian divide.

But now, after the return of peace to Northern Ireland as a result of the Good Friday Agreement, nearly ten million tourists a year make their way to Belfast and the United Nations was moved to declare it the second safest city in the world to visit.

Nowadays television crews make a daily pilgrimage to the renamed Peace Wall to film visitors writing messages of hope and reconciliation. Nonetheless, unlike Berlin, where the wall that divided the city is gone, Belfast's 25-foot-high wall is still in place and every night the series of steel gates dividing the Catholic and Protestant communities are still locked.

Local taxi firms do a roaring trade with political history tours. Orange and green leaflets proclaim: 'There are two sides to every story. Up the Shankill… down the Falls. Write your own message on the Peace Walls.' There are mural tours that take visitors to view the iconic wall paintings illustrating a city that was torn in two.

Catholic taxi drivers going into the Protestant areas warn passengers, 'When we are on the *other* side, don't call me Patrick. My new name is Ken.' One tour visits Milltown Cemetery, where in 1988 Loyalist fanatic Michael Stone gunned down three mourners and injured at least fifty others at a Republican funeral.

Republican martyr Bobby Sands, who died on hunger strike in Long Kesh jail, is buried here, alongside others who died fighting against British rule, including Siobhán's school friend Mairead Farrell, one of the three IRA activists shot dead by the SAS in Gibraltar in the same year as the Milltown masacre. In this Republican burial ground the martyrs' graves are laid out military style beneath a huge monument over which flies the Irish tricolour. Siobhán's father, John Kilfeather, also reposes in this graveyard which lies in the shadow of the Black Mountains. On one gravestone the epitaph reads: 'Our revenge will be the laughter of our children.'

The position as tutor in the English department at Queen's University, Belfast, was one that Siobhán had long wished for. Her husband Peter was also at Queen's, studying for a film degree. Her daughter Constance was being educated at Siobhán's old school, Rathmore Grammar, and already showing signs of emulating her mother's academic achievements. Her beloved little boy, Oscar, was flourishing in an excellent primary school and probably also destined to attend Rathmore, which was now co-educational.

It was one month before her husband's fiftieth birthday that Siobhán died, but with remarkable prescience she had held a surprise party for him six months before. 'No way you would discover it at that time – you wouldn't be expecting it,' she explained when he challenged her. Peter treasures the expensive white guitar – a Gretsch White Falcon – she presented him with in front of a huge gathering of family and friends.

Siobhán made excellent use of the seven years'

grace that she won for herself by that personal plea in Lourdes. Seven years earlier, on the day she had locked her room at Sussex University with the disease hanging over her, she had said to herself, 'I don't know if I will ever unlock the door again.'

At Queen's University's School of English Siobhán's photograph still retains its place in the glass-fronted faculty noticeboard. It is a steep climb up the four floors past brightly painted yellow walls to the attic at the top of the building.

On the top landing there are framed old black-and-white cinema posters from the 1940s. In predominant places are posters for *Black Narcissus*, a classic nun's story, and *I See A Dark Stranger* – in which, according to Siobhán, 'Deborah Kerr gives a comic rendition of a passionate Irish nationalist who becomes a German spy but is "saved" by her friendship with a British officer, played by Trevor Howard.'

The nameplate on the door reads: 'Dr Siobhán Kilfeather.' Inside, the office is cluttered and cosy with an assortment of armchairs for the comfort of student tutorials. A white Apple Mac computer and a microwave compete for space on an old battered wooden desk.

A beautiful white-painted rose window looks out over the bustling street below and onward to the

Black Mountains overlooking Belfast. A dormer window frames views of the campus and the university's majestic gothic main building. At the back of the room, under the window stands an old wooden rocking chair complete with blanket.

In healthier times Professor Kilfeather was known to advocate the rejuvenating properties of an afternoon nap. Latterly, as her health deteriorated, often the only way she could complete her teaching and research work was to conserve her energy by taking regular breaks and lying down.

Siobhán's attic office was a home from home with pictures of her children and, mysteriously, several cuddly toys. Even her children have outgrown these comforters. Siobhán had not. On the walls, looking for all the world like family portraits, are black-and-white photos of Jean-Paul Sartre and Brendan Behan.

The packed noticeboard still holds reminders about Irish Women's Writing History lessons and a timetable for a symposium Siobhán was due to chair.

Files and boxes are stacked high and everywhere books, books and more books. They spill off the shelves: *Poets of Paris* by Andre Beucleur, *The Works of James Joyce*, *The Irish University Review*, *Diaries of a Dying Man* by William Souter and *Dream Team* – the story of Manchester United.

These books are more than a simple reminder of Siobhán's family home and her father's enormous collection of books. These are his books, lovingly preserved after his death and her mother's move to Shropshire. They are back home now in Northern Ireland, housed in the School of English at Queen's. The intention is to establish a collection dedicated to Siobhán's memory in one of the university's library buildings.

Forgotten, on a hook at the back of the door, hangs Siobhán's favourite coat, the black embroidered one with its shocking-pink lining. Forlorn on the white noticeboard, is a small tattered medical card reminding her of appointments at the Royal Marsden Hospital.

Professor Kilfeather has locked her office door for the final time. Songwriter Warren Zevon, a friend from Princeton days who wrote the song 'Werewolves of London', died just months before Siobhán. He too had cancer. Warren bid farewell to the world with a song of acceptance entitled 'My Ride's Here'.

Siobhán could not refuse this time – her ride has arrived so that she may claim her place in heaven.

SIOBHÁN'S STORY: WHAT'S
THE ALTERNATIVE?

When I first went to the Royal Marsden they told me I would be surprised by how many people make suggestions to you about cures for cancer, especially in the complementary or alternative fields, and also through diet. Owing to its long experience as a specialist cancer hospital, the Royal Marsden only endorses current scientific evidence, established and verified through controlled tests.

However, their attitude was, 'You must do what you wish regarding other treatments – but bear in mind that you are under strain already and to suddenly change your life around, to change everything you eat and drink, can be stressful and expensive. There is something to be said for keeping your life as normal as possible – providing of course that you are eating sensibly anyway.'

The one piece of advice they stress is, 'No smoking.' No matter how far advanced the cancer may be, they still advise against continuing to smoke because, as they see it, nicotine is always going to make you feel worse. Fortunately I've never smoked so that wasn't an issue. They also tell us, 'If you're a moderate drinker, go on doing that, carry on tea and coffee and continue eating meat.

We are not aware of any reason to stop you doing those things.'

The Internet offers so much information about different treatments and theories that it is tempting to want to try them all. Though I have great respect for conventional medicine, I know that over the years many scientific theories have been overturned. On the other hand, it would be closed-minded to dismiss all alternative therapies. I'm sure that many are soundly based. I've used alternative medicine where it has suited my temperament, my income and my circumstances.

The most striking thing I found early on was that I really wanted some treatment to ease the symptoms of stress. A builder friend working on the house who had quite a lot of knowledge about local communes and New Age practitioners recommended a therapist. For some time now I've been going to a lady called Judy once a week for therapeutic massage. She explained that she also does counselling and reflexology, and we talked about my illness.

I humoured her by going there and paying £24 a week for what was to me a beauty treatment. It made me feel better – I never thought it did one whit of good medically but I'm prepared to pay and if she thinks it is medical intervention, OK. Lately, though, my feelings have changed and I've come to have great faith in the process.

I've been transformed physically and instead of shying away from the cancerous area of my back, which I had done in hospital, I've been able to look. The surgeon and nurses had asked if I wanted to see the wounds in mirror and I said, 'No way!' My husband Peter would look at them and describe them to me. They sounded horrendous. Now, with the help of Judy, I've been able to look at the wounds for myself.

Instead of trying to retreat into my brain and intellectualise everything, I'm now learning to use my body to mobilise the immune system and try to fight the cancer. It may seem that it hasn't been very successful because I did get the secondary cancer, but it took a lot longer than it might have done and I do feel physically very fit.

Judy went away to Australia for six weeks and while she was gone I transferred to an acupuncturist. I really took a dislike to her, but instead of saying after the first session, 'I won't come back,' I persevered out of social embarrassment. She would say, 'Let's make another appointment' and rather than refuse I kept going back.

I felt that the acupuncture was doing me some good and I have a lot of respect for it. I've had it before and can see a solid scientific basis for it. It makes sense intuitively and from what I know about anatomy it seems to be a reasonably sensible system. It can work for some people, but long term it wasn't for me and I know in my heart that was because I couldn't take to the therapist – so it was the practitioner not the treatment that I didn't get on with.

As for homeopathy, I haven't investigated it in any serious way, but I have a friend and she's a great believer. I've taken some preparations that she has recommended but it hasn't suited me to go to her for a structured course of treatment. In my mind it is a bit like a witch tying a bit of white wool around my leg. I can't see how it could improve my condition, though I know lots of sensible people do have great faith in it. I know it requires a high level of training but it just doesn't suit me. I wish it did but somehow I just blank on it.

My diet came from Cancerbackup. They have a web page and they mail out information to you. When I first discovered the melanoma, my friend Liane [Jones] got me in touch with them and they put me on their mailing list. I could have as much or as little information about my particular kind of cancer as I felt I could handle. Included were details of some of the most widely used complementary and alternative treatments.

The Bristol Cancer Help Centre [now Penny

Brohn Cancer Care] is the most reputable of those who hope to influence the cancer by diet, minerals and vitamin supplements. I was broadly aware of the principles practised at Bristol and their emphasis on vegetarianism and organic foods and certain kinds of therapy.

With hindsight I now wish that I'd gone to Bristol in the time after I'd left hospital and was recovering from surgery. However, at the time I thought we couldn't afford it and I didn't want to leave the children. I thought it would be too much to spend because you are encouraged to be residential rather than an out-patient. Everything I know about them suggests that they have developed a very fine system. So I decided to do what I could at home and one of the first things I did was to alter my diet to conform to their basic suggestions.

One of the things that I am most convinced is essential – and I am almost a missionary about it now – is the need to drink large amounts of water every day. I'd always known it would be a good thing but I'd not got around to following the recommendation of three or four litres a day.

At first I found it very difficult physically to drink that amount of water. You almost have to have a glass of water on the go all day and it does mean getting up frequently in the middle of the night. But the body adjusts and now I drink water all day and stop at about 6pm.

One piece of advice the acupuncturist gave me which has proved helpful is to take a lot of uncooked oil. I've never like oil or fat or margarine or butter but I now take 10–15 milligrams of olive oil a day – not capsules, just straight. It tastes awful but I feel the combination of the oil and the water is good for strengthening the cells.

These are some of the more sensible suggestions but there are other, more wacky ideas doing the rounds which I've read or heard about.

I actually tried what is called Gerson Therapy Diet. The recommendation is to drink raw vegetable juice once every couple of hours day and night and also to take coffee enemas (though I've never tried that). But I do know this diet – the 'juicing diet' – is the one that has the most cult status at the moment. I knew that I wanted to try it out but it is one of those radical therapies that say that you must refuse chemotherapy and do the diet only and I'm not prepared to do that.

My view is that probably they would be delighted to offer these treatments at the Royal Marsden if there was any possibility of saving every patient from cancer.

Since the secondary cancer appeared, people have assumed I must be desperate and well-meaning friends and colleagues have suggested various fringe methods of treatment.

The Hulda Clark method was recommended to me by a friend from university days. One premise of this treatment by the Californian naturopath Dr Clark is that cancer is caused or exacerbated by parasites in the mouth and located under your teeth.

I've been given the name of a dentist whom I'm told will remove all your teeth as a cure for cancer. My first thought was to consider it as wacko, but then I began to tell myself that there might be something in it because I've had terrible trouble with my teeth since I've had cancer. Perhaps I shouldn't have had some root-canal work I'd undergone some months previously.

It now seems to me that possibly my immune system is compromised and that the teeth problems and even my earache are to do with the cancer. The Hulda Clark method also tries actively to destroy parasites in the body. I have this little electronic zapper and a box that flashes a green light and two little prongs and I sit in front of this for an hour a day supposedly 'zapping the cancer' while the light winks up at me.

I can't see what it is meant to be doing, but as it seems to be quite harmless it's tempting to sit there all day long. I hope I'm not doing it an injustice because

I haven't really studied it. However, it does seem to be based on an act of faith rather than real science.

The Hulda Clark method was also related to the gift I received from a friend – a bottle of a mystery liquid called Planet Solution. The instructions here recommend washing all fruit and vegetables in this solution as well as putting it in the dishwasher and washing machine, washing down walls and work surfaces with it and pouring it down the toilet. Thinking about the latter I rebelled, realising it would be costing around £10 a day!

This aspect of some of these more way-out products concerns me because people with cancer are very vulnerable. Of course if it were a matter of life and death you would find the money – and if I really believed that having all my teeth taken out was going to save my life, I would do it. I would even be prepared to have limbs removed or undergo surgery again if it was going to allow me to live.

I feel able to balance most of these options rationally, knowing that if I decided to spend £10 a day flushing Planet Solution down the toilet we could find the money, even if it meant borrowing from the many friends and relatives who have already offered financial help.

What worries me is that many of the patients I meet on my regular appointments at the Royal

Marsden aren't very well off and many of them are more frightened and alone than I am.

It troubles me that people who are ill and vulnerable might be tempted in their desperation to deprive themselves of comforts and even necessities. Perhaps they will put themselves in debt and make themselves even more ill through stress with these kinds of possibly false hopes. It would disturb me to think that anyone was borrowing money to try some of these therapies.

The financial price some ordinary people are forced to pay for having cancer is shameful. Many of the patients I've come across during my treatments have lost their partners, their jobs and their homes.

This also reflects on an upsetting situation concerning the National Health Service. Talking to fellow sufferers, it seems to me that many patients feel they would have a better chance of survival if they were able to afford private treatment. I've always believed in the NHS and have been committed to public medicine, but I have to be honest and say that when the time came I asked the Royal Marsden if I could have anything more quickly or more effective if I 'went private'. I was pleased from the point of view of peace of mind – and of course financially – when they assured me that the treatment and medical care would be the same. The only benefit I would have if I 'went private' was a nicer room.

The Royal Marsden would not carry out any treatment on a private patient that they would refuse to a NHS patient. That's not to say that you couldn't go to Harley Street and pay for a whole range of treatments.

Last year I was entered into a clinical trial where I might or might not get the drug Interferon. I asked if I could pay to have the treatment, but they explained that even as a private patient I would still be randomly entered into the trial and there was no guarantee that I would be given Interferon. Of course I could have gone to Harley Street and been given Interferon on demand, but I didn't feel inclined to do that.

I am convinced that its refusal to discriminate between private and NHS patients makes the Royal Marsden a very special hospital. They operate on an ethical basis and for me that is very important. I would not be comfortable feeling that I was getting something denied to others with the same needs, but I must admit I would not be strong enough to resist the temptation to buy myself better treatment if that were an option. Thankfully it is not.

Chapter Eight

An Inside Toilet!

Siobhán's father, John Kilfeather, was the youngest of a family of six brothers born in the Falls Road area of west Belfast in the 1920s.

There was also one sister, the baby, born in 1932, Marie. Just nine when her mother died, leaving the seven children, Siobhán's Aunt Marie is very much the lynchpin of the Kilfeather family.

The brothers have died but Marie is still lively, energetic and capable. A long-time president of her local branch of the Women's Institute and stalwart choir member at the Catholic Church of St Michael's, Marie is a formidable opponent.

Siobhán had stipulated in the choice of hymns for her funeral service that she wanted a traditional Irish air called 'She Moves Through the Fair'. The parish priest informed her husband Peter that, while the music was acceptable, the lyrics were completely unsuitable. Peter did not know why this should be, but was gently informed that the fair maiden moving through the fair was in fact a prostitute. While not wishing to deny Siobhán's choice of music, neither did Peter feel disposed to argue with the dictates of the Catholic Church.

Enter Aunt Marie. When told of the situation, she headed straight for the vestry and confronted the young priest, who, it transpired, was only following orders. The conversation that took place in that holy place is sacrosanct; suffice it to say that when Aunt Marie emerged it had been agreed that her niece's last wishes would be accommodated.

Marie McColgan, née Kilfeather, lived just streets away from the family when Siobhán was growing up. 'From the earliest age you could mark her out as a child of exceptional intelligence. Not that anyone in the family would ever have let her know we thought that. We're Irish – it's not our way to boast,' says Marie.

'Mind you,' she adds quickly, 'all the family were well educated and well read. All my brothers completed their education up to the age of fourteen, which was the school-leaving age in those days.'

Marie too, at her father's insistence, was educated instead of being kept at home to take care of the brothers and father – a common situation in those days in Ireland.

The Kilfeather family would probably have been classed as lower middle-class and one aspect of their housing arrangements clearly spells that out.

'We always had an inside toilet,' Marie says proudly. 'In those days most folks had a privy at the bottom of the garden – we were considered a cut above because we had an inside facility.'

Grandfather Matthew Edward Kilfeather was a businessman who owned a grocery store on the Falls Road – later known the world over as the centre of turmoil in the heart of Catholic Belfast.

'Everyone just referred to the store as "150",' according to Marie. 'That's where Siobhán was born. The shop had become a bakery and when my brother Johnny married Renee, Siobhán's mother, the couple took over the shop and ran it for some years.'

Siobhán's father, John, was a civil servant. 'Never was a man less suited to a job,' says Marie. 'He hated it but there was no way he could give it up. To be a civil servant was considered a plum job – you were set up for life. My father was very proud of Johnny and there was no way he would have disappointed his father by walking out.'

Johnny found escape through books. He collected thousands of them. No visitor to the Kilfeather household could ever fail to notice that the home belonged to a voracious reader. 'It wasn't really fair on poor Renee,' says Marie. 'The whole house was taken over by books. You would have to lift a pile off a chair to sit down – then you'd have nowhere to put them.'

But Johnny wasn't just a collector. 'Oh, no,' says Marie indignantly, 'he had read every one of them. He knew exactly what books he had and could put his hand on the work of any particular author or a specific quotation in a second.'

Johnny especially loved Irish literature, Irish writers and books written in the Irish language. However, he was also fascinated by the knowledge contained in books written in other languages, especially French. Marie remembers him taking French lessons in Belfast's Royal Avenue from a French exile living there.

While Siobhán was still at primary school the family moved house. They stayed in the same street, Stockman's Lane, off the Falls Road, but moved from a large house to a small one. Johnny was reluctantly persuaded to part with some of his collection. He donated over three thousand books to a couple who were starting up a book shop in Andersonstown.

'Years later he would still mourn particular editions or authors he had let go during the house move,' says Marie. 'He treasured each and every one of his books.'

Siobhán grew up to share her father's love of books and learning. 'From when she was a tiny wee thing, no size at all,' Marie remembers fondly, 'Siobhán and her father would be discussing and analysing literature, films, philosophy, ideas. She was taught to read, research, ask questions. Never take anything at face value.

'The family were very proud – though we didn't make a big deal of it – when Siobhán became the first pupil from her grammar school to win a scholarship to Cambridge University.'

Marie points out that the other attribute Siobhán inherited from her father was his great sense of humour. 'But you'd have to be as quick as them to know what they were laughing about,' she tells us.

During the height of the Troubles in the 1970s Marie moved to Dublin with her husband Pepe and their five children and later they went to live on the coast in Portaferry. 'We didn't go to get away from the Troubles,' she is quick to point out, but it was a terrible time to be living in Belfast.

Marie was asked about an incident when Siobhán and her elder brother Myles had to be taken from their home in Stockman's Lane. Apparently there had been threats to burn down the property. Siobhán told how she and Myles had been handed over the barricades to family members.

'That would be Renee's family,' says Marie. 'Renee was on the other side of the divide – her family would have been on the other side of the barricades.'

The story passed down through the years is that a mob did indeed arrive to burn the house down. Johnny Kilfeather stood on his doorstep and defied them to do their worst. The troublemakers left without causing any damage.

Even today Marie is still frustrated that many people in mainland Britain have no idea of the disruptive and life-threatening horror endured for nearly thirty years by the ordinary people of Northern Ireland. 'I get so angry when I hear politicians complain that there are more people claiming sickness benefit in Northern Ireland than in England, Scotland or Wales. 'To be sure, everyone suffered,' she says. 'There are people here now who will never recover. Even if they have no obvious injuries, their nervous systems are shot to pieces. We lived on our nerves the whole time.'

Marie points to Siobhán's mother as an example. 'Renee suffered from terrible panic attacks,' she explains. 'Siobhán too, God bless her, was very nervy. You can't expect anything different from people who lived with the threat of guerrilla war day in and day out for a generation.'

Siobhán avoided telling her family about her illness becoming progressively worse. 'She was very brave,' says her Aunt Marie, 'but I did receive a letter from her in which she talked about her desperate sadness that she would not see her children grow up. It was heartbreaking. We were all devastated.'

Marie tried to reassure Siobhán. 'I have half the country praying for you,' she told her. 'Two of our cousins are missionary nuns and they had their whole convent praying for Siobhán's recovery.'

The fact that Siobhán was given a reprieve from her cancer after a trip to Lourdes was no surprise to Aunt Marie. 'She was always a very religious wee girl. Thank God for that – if you are not religious I don't know where you would get the strength when you are coming to the end.'

Already Marie is contemplating her own demise and has told her family of three boys, two girls, twelve grandchildren and one great-grandchild to prepare for her end. 'It can't be far off now,' says the seventy-five-year-old.

Marie was extremely pleased that Siobhán had moved her family back to Ireland before her death. 'Families need to be close to each other at times like this,' she says. 'The only consolation I have been able to bring to Peter is to tell him that He knows best. You can't argue with the one who makes the decisions and chooses the time of your coming and going.'

Marie lost her own husband to cancer fifteen years ago. When Peter told her that he still felt numb from the loss of Siobhán, she consoled him with these words: 'Good – may you stay that way for a long time. It is a blessing. There will be plenty of time to feel the pain.'

SIOBHÁN'S STORY: LIFE IN THE HEREAFTER

Even with the cancer in my system I haven't completely escaped feelings of guilt. My experience at the hospital in Stoke shows me that as an educated, middle-class person I have been advantaged by going to my GP and insisting on being referred to the Royal Marsden.

Not one other person I know in Stoke has been referred to that centre of excellence, even those suffering exactly the same condition as me. It is a privilege to be able to demand to see a particular oncologist – thanks to a telephone call to a friend who was at Cambridge with me. He talked to people in the medical field and they in turn rang around the country to get a recommendation for the best oncologist.

That is an advantage that only those who are wealthy and powerful can exercise. Most people would have no way of discovering the existence of Martin Gore or finding out why the Royal Marsden is the specialist hospital in treating malignant melanoma. I do feel hugely privileged.

It was Mr Gore, consultant oncologist (and now Clinical Director) at the Royal Marsden, who told me, 'I intend to get the Nobel Prize for advances in the treatment of cancer – and I don't intend to lose you to the disease.'

Going back to the initial situation with my GP when he dismissed my claims that I thought the melanoma on my back was malignant, I do feel angry and bitter. There was a time when Peter and I tried to make a joke of it, threatening to summon the doctor at midnight on a spurious call. Of course it wasn't simply one doctor at the surgery responsible for misdiagnosing the cancer. But I do feel bitter that one specific doctor could be so casual about something that was a matter of life and death to a patient.

Had he really put himself in my place and thought of me as a mortal being, the equivalent of his own wife and mother of his children, then he should have behaved differently. It would have meant a great deal had he explained that his conclusion that the melanoma was not malignant was an opinion and not a matter of fact.

What deceived me was that I understood him to be

saying that it was not cancer. With hindsight I am prepared to accept that what he actually was saying was that, in the balance of his opinion, it didn't look like cancer to him.

In America, if you draw your doctor's attention to anything suspicious, they immediately refer you to hospital and have it biopsied and removed. Of course you pay for that and there is a simple issue here. My GP was not being stupid or casual when he said that the mole wasn't cancerous – the fact is that doctors here could not afford to refer everyone with a suspicious mole to hospital.

What I would have liked is for him to have said: there is a ninety-per-cent chance that it is not malignant – but there is a ten-per-cent chance that it is. It will cost you £100 to find out for yourself. Obviously I would have spent hundreds of pounds given the chance.

However, that in itself raises another moral question. Suppose I had been an impoverished pensioner and my doctor offered me that choice? To say to people with no money, we give up the responsibility but, if you want to find out for yourself, then go private – that would be unethical and reprehensible.

So there is no easy answer. I can see that they cannot afford to refer everyone just on suspicion but I do wish the doctors had been more honest with me. Though honesty itself is difficult. If they were straight with everybody, doctors would be frightening people and constantly suggesting that patients go to the private sector.

Mostly I am angry with myself for not being more informed and not taking more responsibility. I think this brings us back to Lourdes – back to the time when I first had the symptoms and what would it have meant if I had been diagnosed with cancer.

The first symptoms arose when I was pregnant. The mole grew and started to bleed. What if they had found out it was cancerous and had offered me a termination. What would my answer have been then?

I'm glad not to have been faced with that choice. Or suppose I had discovered that I had the cancer six months before my mother died instead of six months afterwards in May 1999.

We couldn't have kept it from her. She would have known. The district nurse was visiting, I was in hospital and I was bandaged on my back. So the last months of her life could have been destroyed by the knowledge that her daughter was so terribly ill. Maybe if I'd discovered the cancer it would have saved my life but I'm not sure that is a good enough reason to have given my mother all that worry when she was almost at the end of her life. I'm not sure that would have been a price worth paying.

My mother, like so many of her generation had a

hard life. She had a dreadful final illness. She was a smoker and died in great pain with lung disease. At least she died believing that Peter and I were happy and secure with our young family. She died happy that she was leaving us money to extend our house and have more prosperity than she had even known.

By some twist of fate all that peace of mind could have been blasted away from her. Nothing would have compensated for what she would have suffered in those circumstances. It is pointless to blame the doctors, or be bitter and angry. Somehow in the divine plan it all has worked out for the best.

At the time of illness even more complex questions are raised about the issue of faith. My husband Peter and even some friends do seem to take the view, 'Who would not believe in eternal life when you are dying?'

I mean, surely all of us would rather die believing that our lives had meaning and shape and that we will live on afterwards to oversee and protect the people we love? Surely rather that than our lives are going to come to a complete stop? It's the thought of that annihilation that is so frightening.

I do believe – and I can't explain why – that the way we think of death is really a metaphor. I don't know if I believe in life as we know it after death. Like being in a meadow surrounded by flowers. Just as, in the case of the apparitions in Lourdes, it doesn't seem to matter too much whether Our Lady actually appeared to Bernadette Soubirous and whether she wore a white dress and blue sash. It is a vision expressed as an icon of the late nineteenth century.

Similarly, much of the way we think of death and life after death is in a form of poetry. If one of the things that God's grace does is to allow us to imagine our lives as a story, then that is grace in itself. I can live with that as a kind of redemption. If the only thing that religion did was allow the consolation when dying that there is another life – that would be of little benefit, whether it were true or not. But it is not just consolation because it is not totally consoling. One of the things you are rebuked with when you come to Lourdes is the realisation that one should be like the late Cardinal Basil Hume, who displayed a wonderful example of welcoming death.

If we truly believe the promise of the resurrection rather than just consoling oneself, we should be actively rushing forward to embrace this earthly death and truly believe that this is where true life begins in the hereafter.

During my trip to Lourdes in February, staying at the Hotel Tara overlooking the river, I had a dream. I saw a vision of a circle of stars, or should I say halo of stars, around the Blessed Virgin's head. Shortly before that I had dreamed of having another child –

having previously thought I had extended myself enough in motherhood.

In the dream I talked to Oscar and Constance and said, 'Yes, we can go further. We can embrace another child.' The dream gave me a wonderful feeling of peace and hope that is still with me. It is the promise of a new beginning. A rebirth.

Chapter Nine

Schooldays in a Divided City

At Rathmore Grammar School for Girls in Belfast, Siobhán was firm friends with two other pupils, Deirdre Finnegan and Anne Mitchell.

Siobhán had known Anne since they were infants together at Rathmore Sacred Heart of Mary School, which was linked to the grammar school. She met Deirdre in the second year around the age of twelve, after the first year had been streamed and the top band placed in a new class for high achievers. The three girls were part of a larger group of half a dozen who shared interests in sport and music. Siobhán played violin in the school orchestra and she and her friends were league-topping members of the hockey team.

Belfast in the early 1970s was at the height of the Troubles and the entire population, Catholic and Protestant, lived under virtual siege. Friendships formed during that period were forged literally in an atmosphere of life and death.

Deirdre Finnegan, lifelong friend of Siobhán and now a highly successful Belfast businesswoman, recalls the seriousness of the situation. 'Even in the common room at school,' she says, 'you had to choose your words and your opinions extremely carefully. True, it was a predominantly Catholic senior school, but there were different factions.' Still distressed thirty years on, Deirdre explains: 'We were in constant fear for our lives, waiting for the next bomb to go off, the next riot to start; the tension was terrible.

'Our parents were frightened to let us out of their sight. We hardly were allowed out of the door except to go to school and church. They constantly warned us, "Watch what you say." It was drummed into us, "Trust no one and never, ever go into an area you don't know."'

As schoolgirls growing up in what was virtually a war zone, friends such as Deirdre and Siobhán bonded and clung to each other with a desperation and unshakeable mutual dependency.

'Once alliances were formed, they became lifelong,'

says Deirdre. 'We did not have the freedom of other young teenagers to go out and socialise, meet new friends. In fact, we were rarely allowed to go out anywhere except to each other's houses – and then never after dark.

'We weren't even allowed into the city. There were armed solders and armoured vehicles on every street. Riots, bombings and shootings were everyday occurrences. Even adults who did go shopping in Belfast had their bags searched in every store and restaurant. You were frightened even to go on a bus.'

In the midst of this chaotic existence the schoolgirls maintained some semblance of normality. Their dreams and hopes tended to centre on achieving good exam grades so they could escape to university on the mainland.

Deirdre remembers: 'We spent hours looking at maps of Great Britain and working out the universities that were the furthest away from the Troubles in Northern Ireland.'

Deirdre and Siobhán were members of an elite group at Rathmore specially chosen by the nuns to be 'hothoused' to excel academically. Four were chosen to sit the Oxbridge entrance exam. No pupil from Rathmore had ever reached the heights of being admitted to one of the two most prestigious universities in Britain, Oxford and Cambridge. Of the four who were selected at that early stage, only Siobhán eventually passed the entrance exam and achieved the dream of bringing honour to her school. She became the first student from Rathmore to go to Cambridge University.

It is said that no family in Northern Ireland was untouched by the Troubles. Every family had had someone killed, maimed or arrested. Even the date of Siobhán's birthday was remembered because 16 August was the day the British Government, under Prime Minister Margaret Thatcher, brought in internment, which permitted opponents of British rule to be held without trial. One particular atrocity left the girls in a state of deep shock. In September 1974 Judge Rory Conaghan, father of a school friend, Mary Conaghan, was gunned down in cold blood by the IRA on the doorstep of his home. 'We were all devastated,' says Deirdre. 'All these years later it still leaves me shaking with fear,' she admits.

Lowering her voice to a whisper, she explains, 'Even now it can be dangerous to say the wrong thing in the wrong place. You never know who is listening.'

Sitting in the luxurious surroundings of one of Belfast's revitalised restaurants, an art deco palace, Deirdre takes a large gulp of water to steady her nerves.

The fear and distress are still palpable – and this in

a Northern Ireland at last enjoying a measure of peace and stability. She is speaking in May 2007, in the week of the landmark handshake between the Protestant leader the Reverend Ian Paisley, now First Minister in the power-sharing parliament, and his deputy, diehard Sinn Fein leader Martin McGuinness.

For Deirdre the nightmare memories of the past are never far away. 'I had been in the judge's house babysitting Mary's younger sister, also called Deirdre, just two days before. We were as close as family and outraged that something so horrific could happen in our own circle.

'They were dark days. Even just telling someone your name could be dangerous.' Deirdre explains that her name would immediately mark her as a Catholic – the same goes for Siobhán. 'Terrible things happened to perfectly decent people. You could just be in the wrong area at the wrong time and become a target. Simply for having the wrong religion.'

One feature of the pupils' out-of-school activities was the highly publicised but inevitably ineffectual Marches for Peace. Deirdre recalls: 'We would be taken from the school still dressed in our uniforms and gather outside Belfast Town Hall in support of various groups who tried with varying degrees of success to form a peace corps. I remember once being given a badge which quoted John Lennon's song "Give Peace a Chance".

'Sad to say, we couldn't even openly wear a badge expressing such a sentiment. There were plenty of people even in our school who had no intention of giving peace a chance.

'It was such a stressful and unsettled time that all of us got sick in some way. We all found different ways of coping.' Deirdre's solution was to stop eating. Suffering from life-threatening anorexia, she was eventually removed from school in the sixth year. An official examiner was provided to allow her to take her A levels in her ward at Belfast City Hospital. 'Even being in hospital did not free me from the danger and tension,' she confides.

While she was glad to see her friend, the judge's daughter Mary Conaghan, Deirdre dreaded the anticipated visit from another fellow pupil – activist Mairead Farrell. Mairead would later gain fame as one of the 'Gibraltar martyrs', the trio of IRA terrorists killed by the SAS while taking part in an undercover operation on the Rock in 1988.

It is impossible to exaggerate the fear and uncertainty that overshadowed the lives of these young Belfast schoolgirls. Thankfully it proved impossible to completely suppress the exuberance of youth. Deirdre laughs as she fondly recalls the joke she and her friends played on Siobhán at her sixteenth birthday party. 'Even at that age, Siobhán always seemed so much more mature than the rest of us. She had an effortless glamour and she was so capable, bright – and switched on.

'We agreed to test her ability to maintain her composure by giving her the most horrible, naff presents, and see how long she could hold out being polite and gracious.' The schoolgirls suppressed their giggles as Siobhán unwrapped a bottle of the most disgusting, cheap perfume. 'Oh, lovely,' she said, wrinkling her nose at the stink. 'Splash it on,' they called gleefully.

Next she unwrapped a hideous ornament. 'We were desperately trying not to laugh and give the game away,' says Deirdre.

Siobhán politely thanked the girls for their thoughtful presents. The list of horrible gifts went on and she must have been wondering if her friends really liked her at all. 'Eventually we relented,' remembers Deirdre, 'and put her out of her misery. Hidden under the table we had her real gifts.'

Siobhán enjoyed the joke as much as anyone. On another occasion the joke was on the teachers. With a mock O-level Chemistry exam imminent, some of the girls discovered that the paper on which they were to be examined was the O-level paper from the previous year.

One enterprising pupil went to the school library, obtained a copy of the previous year's paper and together the friends were able to crib the answers. On exam day the girls worked to a system. Reminding each other of the mnemonic 'Cuddly Bunnies Come Down At Easter' – the first letter of each word cleverly provided the answers to the multiple-choice questions – they confidently sat down to take the exam. They all passed without being found out. Deirdre recovered her health enough to go on and attain a law degree at the University of Kent. The university's location, Canterbury, she explains, was 'the furthest point from Belfast on the map'.

After university she returned to her hometown of Belfast. Although Siobhán moved to America and then Shropshire, the two remained friends.

The girls helped each other nurse broken hearts through Siobhán's on–off romance with Gary Eason and a failed relationship for Deirdre. Regular weekends were arranged in London when the friends were able to catch up all the developments in their lives. However, Siobhán was not able to attend Deirdre's wedding because she was in Paris. Still, she remembered her good friend's special day and Deirdre received a postcard from her which read: 'At the moment you were exchanging your vows, I was in Notre Dame Cathedral, saying a prayer and lighting a candle for you.'

More than twenty-five years later Deirdre was in Paris, celebrating her wedding anniversary when Siobhán was admitted to hospital for the final time.

Although Siobhán was back living in Belfast the two had not been able to meet, though they had tried to set up get-togethers. 'At Christmas 2006 we promised each other we would make a special effort to meet up,' says Deirdre. Instead she was to receive an email from Siobhán telling her that the cancer she thought she had beaten seven years before had returned.

It was noon on Easter Saturday in 2007 when Deirdre visited Notre Dame Cathedral and lit a candle for Siobhán. 'I prayed that she would be taken quickly and not have to suffer for too long.' Siobhán passed away peacefully at that hour on that very day.

Deirdre and Siobhán had a very special brand of friendship. 'We could go years without seeing each other but the minute we met up it was as if we had seen each other the day before,' Deirdre says. 'We would slip into that wonderful warmth of old friends and the years dropped away. It was as if we were still young girls in the common room at school with our feet up on the coffee table.'

Although their roots were in that convent school,

Deirdre says the religion of their childhood did not always sustain them. 'Some of us reacted against the strict discipline of the Catholic religion. Siobhán, though, was always what you would call a "good" girl. Without necessarily being religious, she was an especially kind and caring person. We used to tease her because she did not approve of gossip and would always try to find the best in people.

'When a person dies in their prime, it is sad but Siobhán's presence will genuinely be missed. She was a shining star. Glamorous, beautiful, capable.'

Then Deirdre says, 'Let me share something with you. This is strange. Siobhán was the only one of our group who appeared to have achieved it all. She fulfilled early expectations of getting her degree and having a dazzling career – she also was blessed with a loving husband and two beautiful children.

'Some of her friends believe that, although the end came too soon, for Siobhán it truly was a life completed.'

SIOBHÁN'S STORY: MY MOTHER
AND FATHER

Born: 9 August 1957; Royal Victoria Hospital, Belfast; 11lb 4oz.

The family story goes that I was the largest baby

ever born in Belfast's Royal Victoria Hospital. When I had my own children I realised why my mother had not had another child after me!

I have an older brother, Myles, who was adopted when I was three and he was five. It wasn't that my parents didn't think they would have more children, but they had been making moves to adopt when I came along after five years of marriage. They thought they owed it to God to go ahead and adopt a child.

My mother in particular was very religious, but then I would say that when I was growing up everyone was religious. I don't think family and friends would have considered my parents overly devout because in fact there are relatives much more devout in their religious observances.

However, I think my parents had a combination of religious devotion and strong left-wing political principles that led to a commitment based on social concern, particularly for the poor. I think this was also a motive for adopting.

My mother, Renee, had converted to Catholicism, though she was from a family strongly Protestant and pro-Unionist. Her father had always been a liberal within the Unionist tradition and was an active member of the Northern Ireland Labour Party and very anti-sectarian.

Her family were all somewhat horrified when she first started making moves towards Catholicism. She was brought to the Catholic faith through her political idealism. She had been evacuated in wartime to Cullybackey, which is close to Ballymena, out of which grew Ian Paisley's Free Presbyterian Church. During the war her family had to live in this very strict Presbyterian village where there was no whistling, no riding bicycles and women were not permitted to wear trousers.

Girls had to be girls and everyone had to be at church three times on a Sunday. I think this upbringing began to set her against Protestantism. What drew her to Catholicism was that she was aware through conversations with other youngsters and through listening to her father of the sectarianism and bigotry that was endemic in Belfast.

She joined the Labour Party when she was sixteen and met my father and began to go around with this group of young Catholic boys and girls. They were part of a debating society and my father was thrown out along with his friends for being too communist within the Labour Party. After one particularly heated political meeting my mother walked out in protest and joined forces with this group of exiled Catholic lads.

When she saw the kind of social injustices and prejudices which were all too familiar to them, but foreign to her – having grown up in a different tradition – she was filled with a sense of indignation and became more interested in Catholicism as a religion.

She had been friends with my father and his pals for about three or four years when she came in from work one day with a headache. Without warning, she collapsed and had to be rushed to Belfast's convent-based Mater Hospital. She was diagnosed as suffering from a brain tumour.

My mother was nineteen years old at the time. Her parents were told that there was very little hope of her surviving and that the brain tumour was inoperable. Fortunately, a young doctor in the hospital called Peter Gormley made the decision that it was worth operating on the tumour, though he had to admit that he didn't believe her prospects were good.

When my grandmother heard this, she said, 'Well, she's had a great hankering to be a Catholic – so could we get a priest and have her baptised? I know this is what she wants.' So my mother was baptised on what appeared to be her deathbed. She didn't immediately spring back to life again but, possibly to the dismay of some members of the family, the operation was a tremendous success. After many months in hospital she was allowed back home again.

She was left with a residual deafness and was for ever-more in delicate health – mostly because she lost a lot of weight during her illness and was never able to put it on again; she weighed only about seven stone, though she was a tall lady.

After she regained her strength she took formal instruction in the Catholic faith and was confirmed in 1952, the year of her marriage. She was twenty-five by then and had been friends with my father for over eight years.

She had been christened Rachel Killen Docherty, after her grandmother. Her aunt was also called Rachel and the old lady said she didn't want yet another grandchild with her name. She would rather she had been called Renee. I think it was the name of a popular film star of the time. Grandma started calling mum Renee as a nickname. Although some members of her family called her by her proper name of Rachel, for all her life she was known as Renee.

She married my father, John Kilfeather, in a small church in Antrim, north of Belfast. There was a good reason for that, but not a happy one. Some of her own family felt she'd let herself down by moving down a social class to marry my father.

However, that was not the way my father's family regarded it. He was one of six brothers. His mother was dead; his father had been a policeman before the partition of Ireland and now ran a grocer's shop in Belfast. My father had a younger sister who had been only seven when her mother died, and she ruled the roost.

It was this Aunt Marie, according to my mother, who said that nobody from the family should go to my father's wedding. Aunt Marie didn't buy the conversion business and believed my mother still to be a Protestant. My parents were terribly hurt that even my paternal grandfather would not go to the wedding. They went out to a small country parish and were married there in the presence of four close friends. They had a wedding breakfast of bacon and eggs and travelled back to Belfast on the bus.

At that time my father was working in his father's grocery shop. John was thought to be the most clever of his family. Though they were all quite intelligent, John was the bookish one. When he worked in the grocery store this suited him because he passed the day reading books behind the counter.

After the war, thanks to the 1947 Education Act an opportunity arose which had previously been almost unheard of, allowing Catholics to go to Queen's University, Belfast. My father's brothers approached him and said they wanted him to attempt to enrol at Queen's. 'We think you should represent the family and go to university, John,' they told him. They were convinced he was clever enough and had all agreed to defer their marriages so they could support him financially.

My father always said the outcome was one of the worst failures in his entire life. He couldn't take the responsibility and so refused the opportunity to even try to gain a place. Later he explained himself by saying that he couldn't go and feel that all the family's hopes were centred on him. He didn't want to risk disappointing them.

However, he did now realise that his father was anxious for him to make the most of whatever academic ability he had and so he trained as a librarian. He enjoyed the work but felt, rightly or wrongly, that it was impossible to be promoted beyond the most junior levels if you were a Catholic and so he changed careers and entered the Northern Ireland Civil Service. Here it was the same story. It was almost impossible as a Catholic to be promoted. At that time a lot of people in Britain were unaware of this aspect of discrimination in Ireland.

Not only was religion a bar to getting certain jobs, there was also the frustrating situation that those who were employed were left at the lowest levels. My father worked for years in the National Assistance Board and trained people who then rose to be his superiors. He *was* promoted only once in some twenty-five years.

I would have to admit that his own personality probably contributed to that situation. Although he had made a lot of effort in the first ten years, after that he began to take the view, 'Why should I be breaking my neck for the Civil Service and be stuck in this junior position?' So he became someone who just turned up to work, read as much as he could and doled money out to people.

That particular job in the National Assistance Board, though he hated it and it made him very unhappy, produced lots of great anecdotes when I was growing up. It gave him the ability to see the real lives of the poor people of Belfast.

Part of his job was to conduct home visits and he would come back and tell us how difficult it was for ordinary decent people to change their circumstances. He took it upon himself to manipulate the system to get a couple of buckets of coal for elderly people and would ensure that they were put down for a blanket allowance. He also tried to help families juggle allowances to try to get them extra money to raise their children.

The sad lot of the poor gave him a great sense of anger. This may have been what led to his communist sympathies, though I'm not sure if he would have *described himself as a communist. Never a card-carrying member of the party, he greatly admired those who were and always espoused left-wing causes.*

Of course he wouldn't have wanted to be an apologist for Stalinism but, like many other people, he thought the British government exaggerated Moscow's excesses. He was inclined to suppose that things were better under communism than with hindsight we now know to have been the case.

My mother worked in the Civil Service late in her life but when my brother and I were small she took a number of jobs in shops and dry cleaners. She didn't have as good a formal education as my father and at the time he took the Civil Service examinations she wouldn't have been qualified to join, having left school at fifteen.

When we were very small she worked in my grandfather's shop and when he fell ill my parents ran it as a bakery for a few years. As we got older my mother started taking in sewing and doing lots of the piecework jobs that working-class women do. She also worked for opinion poll organisations and for a time was employed as a cleaner for a local Protestant minister. She would tell us lots of stories about how mean the family were.

In truth they were actually very nice and very good to us but their ways were very different from ours. I realise now it must have been a very hard job, though I didn't remember her complaining about it at that time. When I was about seven up to thirteen she worked as a night nurse in the local hospital. She was then able to be at home to look after Myles and me during the day and she would also arrive home from her shift in time to do our breakfast before we went to school.

She had a miscarriage at forty while she was doing that job in the hospital and although she never said anything at the time, now I see that you wouldn't want to be pregnant doing that job. It was a hospital for people who had been injured in the Troubles – wounded soldiers and others with spinal injuries. So what she was doing for a lot of the night shift, along with other nursing auxiliaries, was lifting and turning people in their beds. Not an ideal job for someone who is pregnant.

Chapter Ten

Kindred Spirits

A nne Mitchell is an eminent immigration lawyer in Washington, DC. Her name is legendary among the Irish in the American capital. Irish newspapers have run several profiles on this local girl who came to the States and made good.

She also happens to be Siobhán's closest and oldest friend. The pair have been variously described as peas in a pod, twins or two shadows.

'You never saw one without the other,' explained a school friend. 'Whether they were carrying hockey sticks or violins, there would also be the two of them. They even wore their hair alike.'

As four-year-olds starting at Rathmore Sacred Heart of Mary School in Belfast, the two immediately became best friends.

One incident that sticks in Anne's mind concerns their early religious upbringing. 'One particularly zealous nun, Sister Marie, was telling us children in the first year about St Theresa, the Little Flower, who was tortured and killed because she would not denounce her Catholic faith. Sister Marie was determined to get her message across and used a particularly graphic example. '"If a masked gunman were to rush into this classroom now," she said, "and offer you sweets if you gave up your faith – threatening to shoot you if you didn't – would you sacrifice yourself?"'

Anne and Siobhán, the two brightest girls in the class, as always sitting next to each other in the front row, exchanged shocked looks. As if in silent agreement, they answered in unison: 'I'd take the sweets.' Sister Marie was disgusted by her young heathen charges, feeling that she had failed to impress upon them how glorious it would be to die as martyrs. 'She decided we were lost causes and moved us to the back of the class,' says Anne.

'Given everything that was to happen later in our city, I'm still amazed that she would have been so stupid as to offer us that challenge.'

However, the incident cemented the friendship between the two young convent girls.

'There were about ten of us in each class in those days,' recalls Anne. 'We stayed at Rathmore through primary school right up to sixth form. Can you believe it? Over twelve years wearing that navy-blue uniform and they still have that same uniform today. Now Siobhán's daughter Constance is wearing it.'

Anne remembers Siobhán as a fiercely independent character. 'Very much her own person. She never bowed to peer pressure and was so confident that she would even stand up for herself to adults.' Even if it put her at a disadvantage.

Anne remembers going with Siobhán to the cinema on the Lisburn Road to see the violent Western *Little Big Horn*. Siobhán argued that as they were under fourteen they did not need to pay full price. Unfortunately, hearing her argument, the box office manager was able to refuse them entry because they were underage.

Their local Catholic church, St Bridget's, was on the same road. Every Sunday, for all of their childhood, the girls would meet at Mass and then spend the day walking up and down the Lisburn Road. 'We'd walk from her house to my house and then turn around and walk back again. Goodness knows what we talked about,' says Anne.

Perhaps they talked about the books they were reading. Siobhán found a list, *The 100 Best Books Ever Written*, and she decided that the two budding academics should start at No. 1 and work their way through to 100.

'We would be about eleven at the time,' recalls Anne. 'I think I got up to about No. 10 in the list – *Vanity Fair*. Siobhán, I have no doubt, read all 100.'

Anne still recalls how intimidated she was when visiting Siobhán in her house in Stockman's Lane off the Falls Road. 'She had a big black snarling brute of a dog called Tarry and he terrified me,' says Anne. 'Also, her father was not very sociable. In fact at the time I thought he was a grumpy, bad-tempered dad – now I know he was painfully shy.'

Sadly there was a more sinister reason why Anne became frightened to visit Siobhán at home. The Troubles had dramatically escalated after 'Bloody Sunday', 30 January 1972, when British paratroopers opened fire and killed thirteen civilians taking part in a civil rights march in Londonderry. Anne tells of watching British soldiers interrogate suspects in her own city.

'The British Army commandeered a big open field at the bottom of Siobhán's garden. It was in the centre of Belfast and close to one of the Republican heartlands in the Falls Road. They used it as a helicopter launching pad.

'Soldiers used to carry out psychological torture games there. Suspects were brought to the field blindfolded. The helicopter would take off and the suspects were led to believe they were going to be thrown out of the helicopter – if they didn't talk. Most of the time the helicopter was hovering just feet off the ground – but the prisoners were not aware of that.'

The two little girls were silent observers. They would sit in Siobhán's garden watching the macabre games.

'What were we supposed to do,' asks Anne, ' – report them? No, in Belfast at that time it was best not to let on what you knew. Say nothing. Don't get involved.'

Back at school, in their O-level year, Anne and Siobhán developed a crush on the same Irish Language teacher. Neither of them spoke much Gaelic, which put them at a disadvantage. On one occasion when they were late for a lesson, the teacher berated them in front of the class. He called them 'amajack' but neither girl realised they were being called 'stupid' in Irish.

Anne was one of the four girls 'hothoused' at Rathmore Grammar to take the Oxbridge exam, but in the event she decided to go to her father's alma mater, Trinity College, Dublin.

'How was I to know I would be the only Catholic among about two thousand Protestants?' asks Anne. 'Not that it did me any harm – thank God. The sectarian divide we had grown up with in Belfast was not a problem in Dublin.'

While Siobhán went off to Cambridge and then on to Princeton, Anne gained a law degree at Trinity and emigrated to America. After a short-lived first marriage, Anne met and married an American criminal lawyer. The two now share the practice Mitchell Dunn in the American capital.

Anne introduced her husband to her lifelong friend for the first time when Siobhán was in Boston on a book tour with the other editors of *The Field Day Anthology* in 2002. 'My husband is a pretty smart guy,' says Anne, 'but Siobhán blew him away. She was addressing a class of university students and answering questions. My husband, Tom Dunn, told her afterwards, "You used at least five words there that I have never heard in my life – let alone know what they mean." Siobhán grinned and told him, "Oh, I thought there were at least ten."'

Anne last saw Siobhán and the family in their new home in Belfast on one of her regular trips home to see relatives. On a subsequent trip Siobhán was too sick to see Anne but she sent an email with the cryptic message: 'Sick again!'

On the Easter weekend of Siobhán's passing, Anne was in Belfast. 'Even though I didn't see her, I felt close to her. Just for us all to be back home. Later I met up with our school friend Deirdre Finnegan and we held our own little wake for dear Siobhán.'

Anne was comforted by something Siobhán had told her after she came back from Lourdes seven years earlier. 'I didn't go expecting a miracle or a cure,' Siobhán had said. 'I went to ask for acceptance. I found that.' The last email Siobhán sent her closest friend said: 'I'm ready to go. I'm not afraid.'

Looking back to when they were four years old and at school, Anne says, 'Siobhán had her faith to sustain her. I just hope she gets her sweets in heaven.'

SIOBHÁN'S STORY: CHILD OF THE TROUBLES

The Troubles totally dominated our lives. I can't remember now at what age I became aware of the tensions – that there were people we avoided and that those people in turn shunned us purely because of religious differences.

But I do recall from an early age the tension that surrounded the date of the major Orange Marches on 12 July every year. My brother and I would not be allowed out of the house. My parents had moved from the Falls Road, where my grandfather's shop had been when I was about three, and we now lived in a mainly middle-class area off the Lisburn Road.

Our neighbours were almost an equal mix of Protestant and Catholic. We lived in the middle of a set of three houses. The neighbours on both sides were Protestant. The house on the left was occupied by a widower who had several sons and they were in the Ulster Special Constabulary, known as the 'B' Specials. These police auxiliaries – who had a fearsome reputation of violence towards Catholics – were objects of abject terror to us in my childhood.

And for good reason. I remember how my father used to tell his story of the night that I was born. In the true tradition of the 1950s he had not been present at the birth but when he heard that he had a baby daughter – his first child – he celebrated with a few pints of Guinness.

He then made his way up the Falls Road to tell his father the happy news. He was stopped by a member of the 'B' Specials who rammed a gun into his face so forcefully that it had left a mark and said, 'You're lucky I don't shoot you.'

So there was an uneasy truce with our immediate next-door neighbours, the Breeshalls. It's true to say that we were frightened of them. I hated seeing the sons leaving with their guns.

However, on another level they were great neighbours. There were occasions when they offered very practical help. Cousins or other relatives visiting from the country would often bring the gift of a couple of live chickens in a sack. My parents were too wimpish to kill the chickens so we were pleased that Mr Breeshalls would always wring the neck of a chicken for us to provide our roast dinner.

Strange as it seems, we did actually consider them kindly people. Indeed when the real Troubles began, just before British troops arrived in Ireland in 1969, there was a particular night when we were all terrified by the terrible sounds of shooting coming from all areas of the city.

It was the belief of many Catholic families that we were about to be burned out of our homes and possibly murdered. And that wasn't only our conviction. Both of our Protestant neighbours on either side asked my parents, 'Do you want us to take your children somewhere safe?'

It must have been a frightening and intimidating thing for the Breeshalls and it's unlikely that they could have taken the risk. But the elderly couple on the other side thought differently. They drove my brother Myles, who was fourteen, and me, two years younger, up to barricades armed by the IRA and handed us over to uncles and aunts. There must have been no small degree of risk and fear to themselves but they still performed that act of Christian charity for us.

But of course there was always that paradox in Ireland. People had very deep-running enmities and yet at the same time were able to coexist and display great acts of kindness and friendship to people they knew were from the other side of the sectarian divide.

At the time we imagined that we were about to be murdered or lose our homes, this fear was not without foundation. Within our own family, my Uncle Mat, who owned a small pub in Conway Street, was turned out into the street by the Royal Ulster Constabulary and his pub was burned down. So it did happen and proved that our fears were very real.

The Troubles in modern times began in 1969 as a non-violent civil-rights campaign and quickly escalated into sectarian violence. Some 3,500 people died, most of them innocent civilians, and the British Government spent more than £10 billion before finally the two sides of the divide accepted an uneasy truce at the end of the century. Early in 2007 they agreed to share power and the British took a back seat.

Oddly enough, the Troubles and my secondary-school career ran side by side, helping my education in a funny way. From the age of eleven to eighteen, I could count on the fingers of one hand how many evenings I went out.

This was true of most of the people I knew. Parents went through agonies whenever their children were out of the house, especially at night. So we were never part of those days of teenage rebellion when most youngsters would be out at rock concerts or parties or the pub.

You couldn't ignore the fear in your parents' eyes by going out and leaving them with that anxiety. Social life consisted of visiting other school friends at home and we would always be taken by car and collected again. Very infrequently we might get a treat and go to a matinee at the cinema at the weekend.

One of the good things to come out of the Troubles in the 1970s was that there was a lot of cooperation between schools. Several of the local schools and in particular Campbell College, a girls' school, had pupils accepted and their headmaster spoke to me about their experience of preparing pupils to go to Oxford or Cambridge.

However, when I got my A-level results they were not very good and the headmistress was furious. In fact one of the things about Oxbridge at that time was that they had no great regard for the national qualification systems. They made their own judgement independently of examination results.

This sounds arrogant, but I never had been very

good at exams and I thought I knew why. The reason I didn't do too well in A-level English – I got a B: OK but not really an Oxford result – was that the examiners were asking simple questions.

I had read many more books than the syllabus required and consequently my answers were often too complicated. I knew that if I could get past this A-level hiccup I would progress on to the real academics, people who were familiar with wider choices of reading material. They would know the complicated literature I read. I was proved right and that was the case when I went to university interviews.

There was a real feeling that I was also fulfilling my father's ambition – by going to university. However, there was still a conflict of interest because really my father would have liked me to go to Trinity College, Dublin.

As the Troubles progressed my parents, normally cosmopolitan and with broad views, became embittered and far more nationalistic and hostile. Anything English was not acceptable. My father was inordinately proud that I went to Cambridge, but a part of me was aware that really he would have liked me to go to Trinity, where I had been offered a place to read Law. But by then I realised that what I really wanted to do was read English Literature and I took

'Blessed Mary, hear my prayer.' – Siobhán, accompanied by Ellen Jameson, at the Massabielle Grotto in Lourdes.

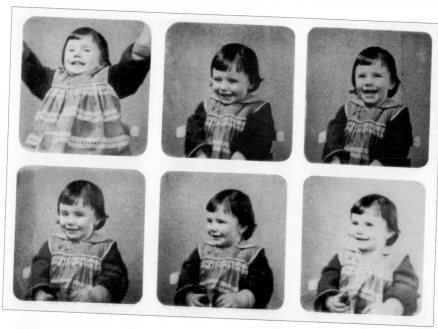

Top: Passport photos of baby Siobhán.

Middle left: 'I've made it!' – Cambridge, 1977.

Above right: Back home in Belfast, 1982.

Below left: Professor-in-waiting, 1979.

Above: Falling in love – Siobhán and Peter in Shropshire, 1984.

Below: Jazz-mad, football-crazy, whisky-drinking Peter.

Above: Marriage in Shrewsbury Cathedral, August 1992.

Below: Celebrating with authors, Derek and Ellen Jameson.

Princeton Professor in the Big Apple.

Hi-tech academic – growing up fast in Cambridge, late 1970s.

Above: Mother and father, Renee and John Kilfeather, visiting Dublin with Siobhán in April 1986.

Below: Father John at quayside shrine, Northern Ireland.

Happily married – stepping out at home, Hope Common, Shropshire.

Above left and above right: The children – Constance, born 1995, Oscar, 1997 – named after Oscar Wilde and his wife Constance.

Below: A sad, final image – Siobhán in 2006.

the view that Cambridge was the best place for that. With hindsight I think Dublin might have been just as good but I can't really quantify that.

Chapter Eleven

An Air of Mystery

Robert Jones, an attractive and softly spoken London business consultant, was a friend of Siobhán for over thirty years.

They met at Cambridge in October 1976. Their surnames started with adjacent initials and the collegiate accommodation system assigned them to adjacent rooms on the same floor in Selwyn College.

'We were also assigned the same tutor,' Robert recalls. 'The Reverend John Sweet, an archetypal Church of England clergyman whose role it was to look after our emotional and secular well-being. Those who were assigned to that tutorial group have all remained friends long after university. It's hard to define what made the Rev. Sweet special but he certainly inspired loyalty in that core group of undergraduates.'

Robert recalls his first sighting of Siobhán in the halls of residence at Cambridge. 'You couldn't really miss her. She was outstandingly attractive,' he says, 'with her dark Celtic looks, black wavy hair, piercing blue eyes and a strangely old-fashioned style of dressing. She was only nineteen but she had an air of mystery – unusual in one so young.

'Siobhán was exotic and entrancing with a captivating Irish accent. Everyone who met her fell a bit in love with her. Many people fell a lot in love with her. However, even those who wanted to get closer were nervous of approaching her. It is no exaggeration to say that many people at Cambridge were in awe of Siobhán. To be chosen as a friend of ours was a high honour.'

Robert was originally studying Philosophy, while Siobhán's subject was English Literature, and he admits that it was probably her influence that motivated him to switch subjects in the third year and join the English undergraduates.

Somehow the combination of Philosophy and English was to steer Robert down a career path that eventually led him to take up his high-powered consultancy role in one of the most prestigious branding and design agencies in the UK, Wolff Olins.

The company was commissioned to design the logo for the 2012 London Olympics. In unveiling the jazzy multi-media image, Olympic honcho Lord Coe answered criticism by saying, 'London doesn't do bland.' Public and media demanded that the ultra-modern logo be withdrawn, even though it had cost £400,000 to produce.

Wolff Olins's offices are in a gentrified area overlooking Regent's Wharf, behind King's Cross Station. The converted fruit-canning warehouse with open brickwork, sleek, polished floors and brightly painted railings could easily feature in the architectural magazines as the ultimate example of a high-tech, minimalist corporate workplace.

Over lunch in the company's fashionable bistro-style dining room, Robert makes a confession. Siobhán did not much approve of the corporate world and certainly not marketing concepts such as branding. Robert, who specialises in defining the qualities that make a particular company unique and marketable, offers a valuable insight into her character.

'She was intellectually self-confident but retained a shyness and naïvety about the big wide world. Her Belfast upbringing during the time of the Troubles meant that she had led a somewhat sheltered existence. But in the world of academia Siobhán's intellect allowed her to comfortably hold her own.

'Siobhán had read more books than anyone else I had met up to that point or indeed since,' says Robert. 'The other students acknowledged her intellectual superiority and her extensive knowledge could certainly be intimidating. However, the other side of her was that she was also shy and a fragile and anxious person. Even back in those early university days I was aware of the two sides of Siobhán.

'She had an endearing humility. She genuinely believed that all human beings are equal and so never behaved as if she considered herself superior.

'Siobhán was perfectly suited to academic life, though her attitudes to learning were considered eccentric. She never took notes in a lecture. "If it's important you will remember it," she used to say.'

Siobhán cultivated several different sets of friends with whom she socialised. Although those friends knew one another, they were not necessarily mutual friends. Indeed Siobhán did little to encourage them to get to know one another. Perhaps this added to her air of mystery or simply facilitated what one fellow Cambridge student described as 'her intense desire for privacy'.

At Cambridge, Robert and Siobhán were enthusiastic members of the theatrical set. They joined the dramatic society and travelled to

Scotland to take part in the Edinburgh Fringe Festival. 'We presented three plays at the Fringe in the late 70s,' recalls Robert. 'One play was called *The Island* and was written by the playwright James Saunders. The second was written by a friend and fellow student of ours and was about an American bomber crew. The third was a play about the tragic poet Sylvia Plath. Siobhán was a behind-the-scenes person rather than a player on stage. I was director and she was assistant director. We all enjoyed ourselves enormously and thought we were producing great art.'

Laughingly, Robert admits that view might not have been the popular one. 'What I remember most is that we had no audiences. Nobody came to see our performances.' At the time Robert and Siobhán were staging their productions, the more famous Cambridge Footlights were nurturing at least two future theatrical giants.

Robert says proudly, 'Stephen Fry and Hugh Laurie were in our college at that time and they were leading lights in the Cambridge Footlights. However, I don't think that either Siobhán or I ever harboured thoughts of making a career out of drama. Siobhán was very clearly going to be an academic and I had set my sights on the corporate world.'

There were others at Cambridge at that time who

seemed to know from the outset what career path they were going to take. The MP Simon Hughes, for instance, was already destined to become a politician. Siobhán too was political and joined many student committees, including the debating society. 'She had a political maturity from all her years of living with the Northern Ireland situation. Siobhán took charge in the political committees and while inviting students to take part in debates would indicate, "I shall chair." We all thought she was terribly assured and grown-up,' says Robert.

However, lest the legacy of Siobhán's university days should seem to be exclusively one of serious debate and academic brilliance, Robert also reveals another side to her. 'I don't remember her as being a super-serious student,' he admits. 'Her social life was, however, always very important. In fact as well as not taking notes she often didn't bother to go to lectures. She was so well-read that she knew already how to compare work, analyse texts and offer critiques. She wrote brilliant, well-researched essays and always achieved high marks – and appeared to do it all effortlessly.'

During the Easter break of 1977, Siobhán invited Robert to accompany her home to Belfast.

Robert was amazed by her family tradition. 'Her parents lived in a very ordinary 1930s suburban semi that was literally filled with books – and I mean filled. Not just on shelves like a normal household. In the Kilfeather home there were piles of books on every surface, on the stairs, on the floor – you even had to weave your way through towers of books to get to the toilet.

'Her father was polite, but not easy to get to know. John Kilfeather was very knowledgeable about books and writers but he was not a fluent communicator. Her mother, Renee, was the opposite. She was articulate, outgoing and immensely interested in everyone and everything. The family seemed to have opinions on every subject under the sun.'

Siobhán entertained romantic notions about Robert at that time but, as he candidly points out, he was 'not for turning'. Still, his long-term partner, Neil McKenna, is convinced that Siobhán had set her cap at Robert. 'Why wouldn't she?' he says cheerfully. 'Robert is good-looking, intelligent, successful – and rich.'

In fact there was no shortage of suitors in her life and, perhaps to cultivate an image of herself as a tragic romantic heroine, Siobhán was forever falling in love, getting engaged and breaking it off. According to Robert, she always had plenty of boyfriends despite a long-term relationship with one of her fellow students, Gary Eason. 'Gary and Siobhán were one of the most established couples on campus,' Robert recalls, 'but the relationship did have an on–off quality.'

He reveals mischievously, 'Her love life was torrid and intense – she loved the drama of it all and I was the shoulder to cry on. However, I did sense on a deeper level that she was looking for the ideal partner. She was extremely attractive and so had no trouble attracting admirers. Most of them seemed, though, to be overawed by her and it was difficult for her to make the right romantic connections. Her standards were very high.'

Robert remained a constant and good friend and visited Siobhán during the two periods when she studied and taught in America, first at Princeton and than at Columbia. 'We had wonderful vacations in New York,' he says, 'enjoying the bohemian lifestyle of culture, literature and the visual arts. Siobhán was always a witty and entertaining companion.'

While she explored life in America, Robert stayed on in Cambridge. 'I was fast becoming the perpetual student,' he admits, 'having completed my English degree, then a Philosophy PhD.'

Still in Cambridge, Robert then joined his first corporate design company and subsequently transferred to London. On her return to England in

1990, Siobhán moved into Robert's London flat in Granville Square, Islington. The impressive building had high ceilings, a grand reception area and a series of small guest bedrooms. Siobhán quickly made herself at home. She was hugely sociable and loved inviting friends round, cooking for them and enjoying lively dining-table conversations until the early hours of the morning.

Siobhán's life was in transition. She had left America to take up a teaching post at the University of Sussex, believing that her elderly parents needed her closer to home. She had also started a serious relationship with her future husband, journalist Peter Jameson.

Robert had also met the man who was to become his life partner, Neil McKenna, also a journalist. The two had been introduced at an Islington watering hole called the Bell. 'I was underwhelmed by most of Robert's friends,' Neil admits. 'Most of them seemed to be drunks or homophobics.

'The first time I met Siobhán was at her wedding to Peter in Shrewsbury Cathedral in Shropshire. Robert was acting as the father of the bride and giving Siobhán away as her own father, John, was not well enough, having recently suffered a stroke. Days before the wedding, Siobhán sent a fifteen-page fax detailing all the arrangements she wanted implemented. I immediately thought, "How anal is that? I don't think I'm going to get on with *her*!"'

But he was wrong – from the day of the wedding in 1992 Siobhán and Neil became firm friends. 'You never got bored in Siobhán's company,' he says enthusiastically. 'You never grew tired of her – she was a very strong life force, a warm, generous, exciting energy. She loved life and encouraged others to enjoy life abundantly.'

Having finally realised that there was not going to be a romance between herself and Robert, Siobhán set about finding him the perfect partner. She had also been instrumental in persuading Robert to 'come out' to his parents. A revelation that he now says changed his life – for the better.

Siobhán had encouraged Robert to discuss his sexuality and he started to see a therapist. During the winter of 1990 the therapist suggested he should tell his parents that he was gay. Robert had his doubts that this was the right course of action. Siobhán agreed with the therapist. Supported and encouraged by Siobhán, Robert arranged to visit his parents at home in Canterbury.

'On the midwinter day that I was due to confront my parents and "come out" it started snowing and I got cold feet. I wanted to avoid the situation and so started to fret that the trains would not be running,' remembers Robert. 'Siobhán wouldn't be put off – she said I needed to follow through and go and tell my parents. It was a turning point, a pivotal point in my life, and I am so as grateful that she supported me.'

Siobhán always took a great interest in her friends' love lives and considered herself something of a matchmaker. Although she did not choose Neil for Robert, she did approve and set about ensuring that the relationship would become permanent. Siobhán had long held the view that gay couples should have the same rights as heterosexual couples and believed that not allowing them to be married was unacceptable because it was discriminatory.

To Siobhán's delight, Robert and Neil sealed their relationship with a civil ceremony in London in March 2006 at which she was a chief guest and reader. 'No one was more happy or proud than Siobhán on that day,' said Robert.

One year later Robert and Neil were readers and official organisers at Siobhán's funeral. Neil vividly remembers the course of events: 'After Siobhán had the terminal diagnosis, she called and asked us to take responsibility for her funeral arrangements. The instructions were to be left on her computer to be accessed after she passed on. She had it all planned.

'She also asked me to buy "Memory Boxes" which

she could fill with mementoes for her children, Constance and Oscar. I bought them from a shop in Bloomsbury; they were beautiful – black walnut, made in Germany. In a file marked "Private" on her computer, Siobhán left all the details of how she wanted the funeral conducted. She chose her own readings and hymns.

'She'd thought it through – she knew what she wanted. She wanted to be buried in the graveyard at Hope in Shropshire where her mother is buried. Siobhán was a devoted and loving daughter. Even though there had been some tension between the two of them in the later stages of her mother's life, she was always very close to Renee.

'Like most daughters, Siobhán was more like her mother than she would care to admit. Her mother was also an intellectual and an avid reader. Siobhán inherited that love of learning from her as well as from her father. Her mother would happily sit around all day reading books and studiously ignoring the housework. Siobhán was the same. Her parents' home and her own were very relaxed and casual.'

Neil suggests that Siobhán would have liked to be more organised but she always seemed to have other priorities. With sadness he recalls times when she would phone him in tears because of the stress of holding down an important teaching post at Sussex University in addition to running a house and bringing up two children.

Peter tried to help, but they were both busy people desperately trying to juggle the demands of home, career and family. Neil tries to define the differences that appeared to make Siobhán and Peter an uneven match. 'Pete tends to be a bit of a Mr Micawber. He is the eternal optimist. Siobhán was a worrier. I would hesitate to call her a depressive but she was inclined to introspection and melancholia. I believe that was a legacy of her Celtic heritage – the troubled Irish history of death, blood, war and ruin.'

Her friends recall that Siobhán was given on occasion to high histrionic camp. It seems that from her father she got the introspective side of her nature and from her mother an emotional instability that displayed itself in melodrama.

Peter agrees and admits that he and the children would laugh at Siobhán's over-the-top reactions to certain situations. They fondly compare her to a character in the comedian Catherine Tate's television show who screams and falls apart when perfectly normal things happen – like a toaster popping up.

Her school friend Deirdre Finnegan offers a more telling explanation for this hysteria. 'Growing up in Belfast during the Troubles we lived under a regime of pure terror and constant tension. We were all scared out of our wits. You don't ever really recover. We are all still waiting for the second shoe to drop or another bomb to go off,' she says.

Siobhán built up a strong and enduring network of friends and supporters to help ease the anxieties she experienced. Neil and Robert were like family to her – especially after both her parents had passed on. They supported her emotionally and often financially. Neil and Robert are guardians to the children, Constance and Oscar, who were twelve and nine respectively at the time of their mother's death.

'Just before Christmas [2006], Siobhán called to say that the cancer had come back,' Robert recalls. 'She asked if she could come visit and stay overnight before her appointment at the Royal Marsden Hospital in Chelsea, London. Siobhán had several friends in London with whom she stayed. We always knew she was inclined to stay with us when things weren't too good. We comforted and cosseted her. We spoiled her. Cooked dinner for her and tucked her up in bed in our spare room.'

Neil went to the Royal Marsden with Siobhán for the appointment in Christmas week. He reveals her obvious distress at that time, just days after the return of the cancer. 'Siobhán was on five Valium a day, so she was not even fully engaging with us.

However, even with her reduced perception she was still able to make intelligent conversation. She had a black sense of humour. We shared that. We were cracking jokes in the waiting room to keep our spirits up.

'We waited four hours at the Marsden. The medical staff had given Siobhán an emergency appointment and she was the last to go in to see the doctor. She was in such distress that day, terrible, awful, falling apart.

'After seeing the doctor she came out of his office looking distraught. The surgeon had said he was going to operate to remove a lump in her breast and one under her armpit. The poor girl was petrified.'

That appointment at the Royal Marsden was on Wednesday, 21 December 2006. The next day she got the results of her X-rays. She returned home to Belfast, where she was now teaching at Queen's University, to tell her husband and children the results.

Coincidentally Neil and Robert bumped into her at Euston Station, where she had gone to catch a train to Manchester and then a flight to Belfast.

'Thankfully she was feeling so much better,' says Neil. 'She had been examined by one of those incredibly confident and optimistic surgeons. He had told her, "I've done hundreds of these operations. Don't you worry. We'll cut out the cancerous cells and if they come back, we'll cut them out again. I have one patient who has had seventeen of these operations. You'll be all right.'"

On New Year's Day 2007 Siobhán flew to London from Belfast and spent the night at her home from home, the Highbury house of Neil and Robert. Neil again accompanied her to her appointment at the Royal Marsden. 'Siobhán had become most concerned about the infection levels in hospitals and so brought her bottles of Dettol and several packets of antiseptic cloths. She kept wiping things down and cleaning everything in sight. That was a bit quirky. She was diverting all her worries into the thought that she might pick up an infection.

'She came back to us after the operation – and of course there was a drama! The drain came out of her wound at midnight. We called the hospital panicking and they said they would fix it when she went back the next day.' There was nothing else for it: Neil applied an emergency patch while Siobhán laughed hysterically – through her tears.

After the operation at New Year, Siobhán slipped into a physical and emotional decline. She had no appetite and no energy. Her close friends were desperately worried. Within days the hospital gave her the prognosis. Her illness was terminal.

Neil and Robert were amazed by her response.

Suddenly a huge change came over her and she took control. From somewhere she drew on reserves of strength. She contacted a solicitor to draw up wills for her and Peter. They agreed to make Neil and Robert and two other friends, Liane Jones and Jamie Buxton, legal guardians of the children – Oscar, named after Oscar Wilde, and Constance after Wilde's wife.

Robert and Neil had always taken an interest in the children and their education. Now they determined to set up an education fund to ensure that both of them would be financially independent to go to university when they are ready.

Trying now to focus on happier times, Robert and Neil recall holidays the family took together. 'We spent a great holiday with them last year,' they reminisce. 'We stayed in a flat at Bishop's Castle, near their home in Shropshire where they lived before the move to Belfast. There wasn't a cloud in the sky. Siobhán was well and fit, the family were fine and we all considered ourselves well blessed.

'We treasure those lovely summer days. Perfect days of memory when the sun shone and friends could enjoy each other's company and all was well with the world.'

There was one other special place that Robert and Neil had shared with Siobhán. They had discovered a healing sanctuary called St Winifred's Well at Woolston in Shropshire. After she came back from Lourdes in 2000, Siobhán made up her mind to take her daughter Constance to St Winifred's to give her an understanding of the sense of peace to be found in a spiritually uplifting setting.

Following her return from that life-changing visit to Lourdes, Siobhán explained to Robert and Neil all about the spiritual work and rituals she had undergone there. 'We had been praying that Lourdes would deliver her a miracle,' says Neil, 'or at the least some healing strength. The situation had been desperate before she went on her pilgrimage to Lourdes. We knew that she had been diagnosed with seed tumours in her lungs.

'On her return – they had gone. There were only three possible explanations: a) that the Royal Marsden had misdiagnosed; b) that her immune system had suddenly activated itself against the seed tumours; or c) that a miracle had taken place.

'We believed it was a miracle.

'On the day of the appointment at the Marsden following her trip to Lourdes, Siobhán came to stay with us. There was much jubilation as we all believed she had been cured. There could be no doubt that she had been delivered by a healing grace.

'On reflection,' says Neil thoughtfully, 'my feeling

is that she was given a divine dispensation. She had made a deal with God to give her more time to bring up her children. I had a feeling that she would get through the first bout of the cancer – but my perspective was that she might well not survive the second. She had always been profoundly grateful for the extra years she had after the Lourdes experience.'

When the initial cancer – a melanoma – had been diagnosed a year before, Robert and Neil paid for Siobhán to have complementary treatment. One that seemed to have beneficial effects was an injection made from mistletoe.

During the last stages of her disease, Siobhán received regular deliveries of homeopathic concoctions from an in-house homeopath, Gilbert, at Robert's office.

She had already made all the lifestyle changes she could make and there were no other adjustments possible. It was out of her hands. Concerned friends, Robert and Neil funded lots of different alternative treatments as a supplement to her conventional treatment.

'We wanted to support her in any way possible,' they explain. 'If the alternative treatments did no good, they at least did no harm. Some of them, especially the therapeutic massages, made her feel better and gave her aching muscles some relief.'

Neil is perfectly candid about reasons for trying to relieve Siobhán's distress. His mother died of ovarian cancer some thirty years ago when she was in her fifties. 'I will never forget the face of one nurse who refused my request to give my mother another dose of morphine to relieve her pain. She said, "We can't, she might get addicted." Days later my mother was dead.'

Neil was working as a freelance writer for the gay press when he first met Robert – and subsequently Siobhán. He once worked as what he described as a hatcheck fairy at the Paradise Club, a gay haunt.

'Just before meeting Robert I'd spent a lot of time writing a piece for the *Independent* on cannabis cafes in Amsterdam,' he recalls. 'The *Independent* held over the piece and I was stony broke. I was pretty disillusioned with journalism but Siobhán persuaded me to take up my pen again.' In 2004 Neil published his first book, *The Secret Life of Oscar Wilde* (Arrow Books). In the foreword he acknowledges Siobhán's encouragement.

'She was so important in the life of Robert and myself we would have done anything we could to help and support her and her family,' he says.

Always practical, Neil proclaims: 'The last thing you need when you are ill is to be worried about money. The statistics are horrendous detailing the financial misfortune that befalls people who have long-term cancer. So many of them lose their house and their jobs. It's not right. When they are ill, people deserve to be supported. We gladly supported Siobhán. It was a privilege.' Robert enthusiastically agrees, paying tribute to the girl he first met over thirty years ago. 'She was everything a best friend should be, concerned yet non-intrusive. She had a unique worldview. She viewed everything through ironic eyes. "Witty intelligence" sums her up perfectly.

'Let me give you an extreme example. It was on almost the last occasion we saw Siobhán alive, Christmas 2006. Her cancer had returned with a vengeance. Somehow we all seemed to sense that the first round seven years before had been an outage. This time there was inevitability, though we all tried to cling on to hope and stay positive.

'The three of us sat comfortably together on the settee at our London home watching a puerile comedy programme called *The Worst Christmas of My Life*. Siobhán was enjoying it enormously and laughing hysterically.'

Finally, in a quiet voice, she asked, 'Do you think Last Christmas of My Life qualifies as Worst?'

Robert and Neil were on a delayed honeymoon in Venice when they got word that Siobhán had died.

Robert sums up: 'We had sensed that the curtain was coming down. Siobhán had been granted an extra seven years of life through divine intervention – now her time had come.

'Her life had been abundant and filled with love and laughter. She also brought those qualities to the lives of other people. Her spirit will live on.'

SIOBHÁN'S STORY: GOING NOWHERE FAST

On leaving school my ambition was to be a writer. I didn't have any clear idea of what kind of writer, but once I got to Cambridge I decided that I'd like to become a journalist because this was a way of being a writer and getting paid for it. I did bits of university journalism and won a prize in a Vogue talent contest in which you had to interview someone and write an essay.

Prizewinners were invited down to the magazine in London and given a smart champagne lunch. The set-up appealed to me and I had the feeling that that was the sort of career I could go into.

That was in 1978 and, in the way that the young are often lacking in self-knowledge, I now realise that no one could be less suited to journalism. I don't have that all-consuming interest in other people, the skills of communication or the ability to meet deadlines. Even at the level of student journalism I was totally miserable. If I was asked to review a book or a play, it was agony, as was anything that involved using the telephone or interviewing people. I just couldn't cope with it. Gary Eason, my boyfriend at Cambridge, also wanted to go into journalism and we were both offered opportunities to train on the Wolverhampton Express & Star. He took it, but I thought, 'Wolverhampton – no thanks.' My attitude was that I'd rather be poor in London than a journalist in Wolverhampton.

After Cambridge I worked in London for some time and did not find my life there easy. I was like a lot of other young people when they first leave university. So insolent that I thought my employer should be grateful to pay me a salary just for turning up and spending my day making long personal phone calls.

The job was in Covent Garden and I was supposed to be a picture researcher. I preferred to wander round the shops and call into the office now and again for a break and a coffee. I was living in a flat with my friend Liane, who was a journalist on the John Lewis in-house journal, and we would get into work in the morning and phone each other several times during the day, usually to make arrangements for our busy social life.

After a period of time my employers decided that I was a luxury they couldn't afford. They let me go and I was deeply indignant at the unfairness of it all. Liane wanted to move in with her boyfriend as we could no longer afford the rent on our flat in Earls Court. The fact was, we spent all our money on gin so we were freezing cold and didn't have enough to eat.

We were living the way people often do when they are young – walking the modest distance from Earls Court to Covent Garden in order to have the money to buy a gin and tonic after work. And there were parties and seeing people we knew. It was quite a fun time, but going nowhere.

During a trip home to Belfast – my father had been ill with the first of a series of strokes – I went to visit friends of my parents at Queen's University. It was suggested that I might like to complete my PhD there as they didn't have many students on their courses. It seemed like a good solution to my living problems and I applied for a student grant. To supplement the course, I took writing classes. Unfortunately my commitment to work had not much improved from the London situation. I did almost no work on the PhD for two years because I spent almost all my time socialising and taking trips abroad.

Eventually my supervisor pointed out that he

was supposed to be able to indicate that I was writing a doctorate since I was getting a grant to do so. Once again I was indignant and astonished. There was only one thing for it: I decided I would abandon the PhD.

My girlfriend Liane and I decided that we needed to make a fresh start in our lives – probably because of some tiff with a boyfriend. We went to live in Rome for a year. We got jobs teaching English to Italian students.

Before we went to Italy, one of the lecturers at Queen's told me that, even though I appeared to be a completely hopeless student, he thought I actually had a little ability and he suggested I apply for a year's study in America. He had gone down this path and drew my attention to Fulbright Scholarships. I applied for one of these to study in America for a year.

While I was living in Rome, Queen's called me back to be interviewed and I was awarded the scholarship – much to my surprise. Since then I have been on the other side of the process, selecting candidates for Fulbrights for students coming from the States to England. Even now I'm still slightly puzzled as to what it was in my ignoble career that they thought merited giving me this scholarship. Still, having been given the award, all I had to do *was get an American university to agree to take me on for a year.*

The PhD that I wasn't making much headway in writing was supposed to be on Samuel Richardson and it so happened that the world's leading authority on this eighteenth-century English novelist taught at Princeton. So I happily wrote off explaining that I had a Fulbright Scholarship and would they accept me for a year?

The letter saying that I had been accepted was delivered to my address in Rome. I packed my bags and headed for Princeton, New Jersey. If nothing else, the trip would be fun while I decided what I was going to do with my life. Possibly because I had no clear idea what direction my career would take, I believed that a year in America would give me more options and ideas.

Once I arrived at Princeton I discovered that education was completely different to anything I had experienced in Britain. All the other students were totally committed, the quality of teaching was fine and study with my tutor, Margaret Doody, absolutely inspirational.

My eyes were opened and I realised that almost every academic idea I'd had in my life previously had been almost complete nonsense. Now I was passionate about my education and convinced that I could do something positive and useful within my chosen field.

I loved the American way of life. I loved the American people, their warmth and hospitality. On my first visit to New York City I was in a lather of terror but also overwhelmed by the glamour and excitement. Yes, the life of an academic was most appealing to me.

Before I went to America I had no idea that the educational system there is so different from the British. If you ask an American university for a scholarship and you qualify, it is quite likely that they will agree to pay all your fees. At Princeton I told the lecturer how sad I was that I had been granted only a year's scholarship. They advised me to apply for a fellowship to finish my education there. That's what happened and I took my PhD at Princeton in 1987. In fact, I wasn't a completely reformed character and I wasn't immediately awarded the PhD because, being lazy, I didn't complete my thesis until 1989. By that time I'd already secured a position on the strength of the part that I had written. My new job took me to Columbia University in New York as a lecturer.

The title of the thesis was 'Strangers at Home' and it was about eighteenth-century Ireland. One of the lessons that Margaret Doody brought home to me, as part of a wider academic movement of that time, was the wisdom of combining academic insights with your personal background and cultural interests and to use that influence in your writing.

Coinciding with my arrival at Princeton in the late 1980s there was a great influence emerging from feminist scholars. They filled me with enthusiasm for women writers. It transpired that little research had been done on Irish women writers and indeed not even much on Irish literature in general – Margaret Doody pointed out to me the benefits of undertaking original work rather than writing yet another dissertation on Richardson, a subject exhaustively covered in the preceding ten years.

My imagination was fired and I was filled with enthusiasm to commence a project that was original and valuable. In that way it happened that I went straight from learning about these specialist subjects to writing about them and lecturing about them.

In the last ten years I've published several essays on eighteenth-century Irish literature as well as work on twentieth-century literature. The writers that I covered in my thesis are a very weird and narrow specialisation so they only have relevance for those academics who are specifically interested in that period of the eighteenth century in Ireland. That being so, I've also written more general work on Richardson and other related general topics.

Since I've been back in England, I've been engaged on massive projects with seven other female academics compiling Volumes IV and V of The Field Day Anthology of Irish Writing, which deal with writing by and about women from Ireland. It's an historical anthology from the earliest times up to the present day. We undertook the project expecting to dedicate a year or two to the work. Instead it has taken over ten.

One of the perks of academic life is to be invited to lecture around the world and I have been fortunate to be invited back to America as well as lecturing in Ireland and all over Britain. After teaching for seven years at Columbia and having contacts at Princeton, I was known by many people who went on themselves to have jobs in other universities.

When they are in a position to pay for a visiting speaker, they often choose one of their friends to come and deliver. That of course happens in all jobs. It's human nature. People prefer to hire others they know can do the job. This means that I'm often invited to lecture in Los Angeles and other American cities because, as well as knowing my subject, I have friends in positions of influence who invite me.

I get asked by many academic establishments to give lectures connected to Irish studies. Partly because a few years ago when I first went to America everyone was very gung-ho about feminism and every other person was investigating women's writing.

In Ireland that influence came much later so the work I was pursuing on Irish women's writing made me more advanced for my generation. There weren't that many people who could undertake the role of lecturing on Ireland and feminism. Nowadays almost every academic conference feels obliged to have someone put forward a feminist position in order to have any credibility.

My passion is research more than the lecturing or writing. My idea of heaven is to spend from dawn to dusk in the rare-books room at the library reading something nobody has read for three hundred years. I've recently worked on some letters in the British Library that a women sent her MP from a debtors' prison in the 1760s. I find it thrilling opening these letters that no other living person has even read and touching the manuscript and looking at the various source material.

If I beat the cancer and survive, I've promised myself that I will really make use of my time and immerse myself in all the aspects of my work which I love.

Siobhán's Miracle

My head constantly buzzes with ideas for new projects. Please God I live long enough to do half of them.

Chapter Twelve

The On–Off
Love Affair

Gary Eason says he was struck by a strange thought as he joined mourners throwing handfuls of earth on to Siobhán's coffin in the village graveyard in Hope.

'It was through me that we were all there together in Shropshire,' he explains. 'It came to me in a blinding flash that I had been instrumental in altering the course of all those people's lives.'

After a two-year romance that started during their undergraduate days at Cambridge, Gary had accepted a place on the journalist training scheme run by the Midlands News Association with its head office in Telford, Shropshire.

Siobhán was offered a place on the same training

course but declined, choosing instead to pursue her postgraduate career in London. She and Gary continued their long-distance relationship and, when he moved into a flat in Wolverhampton and then another in Shrewsbury, Siobhán was a frequent visitor.

Gary and Siobhán met when they both joined Selwyn College, Cambridge, in 1976, the year that the college went co-educational.

A native of Middlesbrough in north-east England, Gary was the first member of his family to go into higher education and subsequently win a place at university. Taking a gap year before going up, Gary was true to his working-class roots and instead of backpacking to some glamorous location, he got a job selling camping equipment at his local branch of Blacks of Greenock.

'I had to lie to get the job,' he says, 'not telling them that it was a stopgap while I waited to go to Cambridge. As it happens, the boss wanted me to train for management and I had to tell him the truth. Fortunately he was very understanding and allowed me to keep my job.'

Cambridge was a world away from the life Gary had known. He found it slightly intimidating, yet he loved everything about it, even though his Teesside accent sounded odd to all those posh middle-class Southerners.

'Looking back, maybe that is why I gravitated towards Siobhán, who also had an accent that marked her out as different. Belfast is similar to the north-east of England. They are both coastal industrial cities – Teesside was built on steel, Belfast on shipbuilding.'

The romance started, as far as Gary can recall, in the summer of 1977. Siobhán and he were in their second year and he had just broken up with another girlfriend.

'Siobhán and I had been part of a group of Cambridge friends that included Robert Jones and Liane Jones [not related]. We were all together at the Edinburgh Festival, where Siobhán and Robert were directing a play on Sylvia Plath at the Fringe. Siobhán and I started dating. The main attraction – apart from the fact that Siobhán was very pretty – was that she was a good listener and provided a shoulder to cry on while I bemoaned the end of my last relationship.'

There was also the undeniable attraction of her academic superiority, what Gary called her 'ferocious intellect'. He explains: 'The whole university system and particularly Cambridge encourages students to think independently. Siobhán was already an independent thinker and she constantly challenged my perspective and assumptions about things. I learned a great deal from her about critical thinking. She was one of the drivers of my new-found intellectual understanding.

'Also, Siobhán was working-class, like me. Through being born and brought up in Northern Ireland, she was also highly politicised. She was intellectually sophisticated and fantastically well-read. As I recall, she read *War and Peace* when she was just eight years old. Of course her father was tremendously well-read.'

In common with Siobhán other friends, Gary has vivid memories of the Kilfeather family's small, end-of-terrace house off the Falls Road in Catholic west Belfast. 'You couldn't move in the house for books,' says Gary with a laugh. 'It was physically difficult to walk up the stairs – there were stacks of books piled up on every step.'

'Siobhán's father was painfully shy,' says Gary, 'and it didn't help that I was Siobhán's *English* boyfriend. His Irish accent was so thick as to be incomprehensible to someone like me. Her mother, Renee, was sweet and also very well-read – if not particularly well educated.'

Gary observes one other thing about Siobhán's father: he was a chain smoker and lived his life in a huge cloud of cigarette smoke. So Siobhán grew up in a house engulfed in smoke – and dusty old books. She herself never smoked, but she did drink wine and loved a drop of Guinness.

While Siobhán pursued her interest in politics and amateur dramatics within the university, Gary was developing his skills as a journalist, working on the university newspaper, *Stop Press*.

'None of us undergraduates really knew what careers we would pursue,' he says, 'but we were taking an English degree so I guess academia for Siobhán and journalism for me were pretty obvious choices.'

Now, over thirty years later, Gary is still a journalist. He has worked at the BBC for more than twenty-five years and now combines information technology with news on the BBC website.

Gary gained a 2.2 in English, of which he was extremely proud. He graduated in 1979 and started work, at the *Wolverhampton Express & Star*, in 1980. He says the fact that someone as accomplished as Siobhán also received a Second shows how tough examinations were back in the late 1970s.

Siobhán subsequently continued her education and studied for her doctorate at Princeton. 'Almost thirty years later one of my strongest memories is of her sitting in my old flat in Shrewsbury typing the application for her Fulbright Scholarship on my old orange Olivetti typewriter.'

By the time the news came through that she had been granted a scholarship, Siobhán had spent time in London living with her close friend Liane Jones, with whom she later moved on to Rome. 'They were typical girls about town,' Gary remembers. 'They rented a flat in Earls Court and then, courtesy of one of Liane's well-connected boyfriends, she and Siobhán moved into a flat in Prince's Gate, Kensington. During the hostage siege at the Iranian Embassy they had journalists camped out in their flat. They charged them for the privilege and thought it was a great wheeze.'

Gary and Siobhán's on–off relationship, which spanned more than a decade, continued with him visiting her in London and later in America, though the pair were never officially engaged.

Still emotionally affected after all these years, Gary admits, 'I don't believe we ever really thought it through properly. It was never seriously my intention to marry Siobhán. However, I accept she probably assumed we would one day make things permanent. It was a strange relationship with us not seeing each other for months on end while she lived in different parts of the world. I was the one always at home in Shropshire and I admit I wasn't faithful. Neither did I really imagine she would be while living on the other side of the world.'

Sounding almost relieved to put his side of the story, Gary owns up to the fact that most of Siobhán friends thought he had behaved badly. He was also the one instigating the frequent and distressing break-ups.

'No one really saw it from my perspective,' he says sadly. 'I was the one who was always being left. Siobhán seemed to take it for granted that I would be waiting there for her when she was ready to come home and settle down. I didn't see it that way.

'All through our relationship I was seeing other people and I even lived with a girl in Shrewsbury. Don't forget, we were still in our twenties, fresh out of university. How could we really know what we wanted in a life partner?'

Siobhán did not appear to have any such doubts. On more than one occasion she asked Gary to go and join her in America, but he was quite happy living in Shropshire and by now working on the *Shropshire Star*. A fellow sub-editor was Peter Jameson and he and Gary were close friends.

Gary did visit Siobhán when she spent five years studying at Princeton up to 1988 and later two or three years teaching at Columbia.

'She certainly had a great lifestyle,' he says. 'Princeton was a lovely town and she had a delightful little prefabricated home which at one time was part of a military barracks on the south side of the town. When she moved to Columbia, her university accommodation was in a very fancy apartment block in Claremont Avenue, close to Harlem. It had one of those awnings out on to the sidewalk to keep the rain off while you walk to the kerbside to get a cab. The Upper West Side block even had a uniformed doorman.'

It was while Siobhán was in America that Gary remembers they were particularly close, although separated physically. 'I used to record love letters on cassettes and send them to her,' he says. 'I would speak the letter and record some of our favourite music – a silly romantic gesture to show her how much I loved and missed her.'

It was Siobhán who found him a job at the BBC. She had spotted an advertisement in the *Guardian* media section and suggested he apply for the job as a sub-editor. He was the successful applicant and moved into a flat in West Hampstead.

One of Gary's favourite pastimes was photography and he treasures photographs of Siobhán he took when they travelled together in America and various parts of Europe. 'We had wonderful romantic holidays in Paris, Rome and Crete,' he says. He also hired a huge Plymouth Valiant from Rent-a-Wreck in New York and spent time driving in the States.

Gary chooses his words carefully when he describes the circumstances of their last parting. 'Siobhán had always been a very nervy person,' he says. 'She could also be volatile and she took our final break-up very badly. It seems that, almost unbeknown to me, she had it firmly fixed in her head that we would marry, have children together and presumably live happily ever after. She took it for granted. Perhaps she should have checked what I was thinking and feeling.'

Although the parting of the ways was his decision, Gary admits that it left him distressed and feeling low.

'I was determined not to put myself through the emotional trauma again,' he says. 'I deliberately cut myself off from all our mutual friends and determined to get on with the rest of my life. Siobhán received all the sympathy but the truth is that I was also badly affected by the break-up.'

Gary did, however, maintain his friendship with Peter Jameson and says emphatically that he was quite happy about him forming a relationship with Siobhán. 'Peter had been besotted with Siobhán from the first time they met. I welcomed them getting together. Mind you, he didn't let the grass grow under his feet after our final break-up.'

Later Gary would marry Stephanie; they have two children and live in High Wycombe.

'Through the years we maintained a Christmas-card friendship,' says Gary, 'Siobhán never really forgave me and it would be true to say that our relationship was distant. However, we are all civilised people, so we did stay in touch. Stephanie and I even visited Siobhán and Peter in Shropshire.

Gary heard the news about Siobhán's illness, first time around, when he received a letter from her and Peter. 'They wrote to their friends and asked them not exactly to pray for them, but at least to hold Siobhán in their thoughts and offer moral support.'

Ever the sceptical journalist, Gary does not mince his words: 'Frankly I thought they were being melodramatic suggesting Siobhán was about to die. Out of curiosity, I asked a colleague on the Health Desk at the BBC, "What can you do about a malignant melanoma?" He shook his head and said, "Don't get one... It's very bad news."'

Gary was at a National Union of Teachers' conference in Harrogate when he received a phone call from a mutual friend informing him that Siobhán had died that day.

'It hit me hard,' he says. 'I felt horribly distressed and being there on my own in a hotel room far away from home – I really was seriously upset. I sat in my hotel room staring out of the window and crying – darkness fell and I just sat there without turning on the lights. The memories of our time together were being replayed on a screen in my mind.

'Happy, joyful memories of two young people who were in love. I felt a great sense of loss. I'm not a religious person but I do believe Siobhán lives on through memories we shared.'

Sounding more poetic than he would probably choose, Gary reflects: 'The graveyard in Hope overlooked by the hills and the Shropshire countryside is a wonderful place to look out on eternity.

'I experienced a profound sense of being part of a larger whole when I realised at the memorial service that I am for ever connected to Siobhán and her family. I am the missing link that joins all those people's lives together, for ever.'

SIOBHÁN'S STORY: LOVE AND MARRIAGE

It never ceases to amaze me how life seems to be planned by something or someone greater than ourselves. The boyfriend from Cambridge, Gary Eason, took up the offer to train as a journalist on the Wolverhampton Express & Star. From there he transferred to the Shropshire Star and it wasn't long before he was writing to me about the two people he thought the world of on the staff there. One was Peter Johnson, the other Peter Jameson. The first time I came up to Shropshire for a holiday, we had the Johnsons over for dinner and the next weekend we had Peter Jameson.

His then girlfriend Jo was away at college in Liverpool, so Peter came on his own. In what I realise was to become a pattern, he came for dinner, had far too much to drink and couldn't go home. He wouldn't stop talking, wouldn't go to sleep and was still there on our sofa the next morning. That first meeting took place in early 1980.

It was nearly ten years before the relationship with Gary finally finished and Peter and I began to move from being friends to a romantic relationship. Gary and I had a very on–off relationship, not least because I was likely to be off to Ireland, Italy or America. Whenever we were together we did spend a lot of time in Shropshire and the Johnsons and Peter and Jo continued to be our closest friends in the Midlands.

In the year I moved to Princeton, Gary got a job with the BBC in London and he sent me a telegram with the wonderful news. This meant he left his home in Shropshire and took a place in London, but he still continued to go back to visit in Shropshire.

He always said that he didn't find it easy to make such good friends at the BBC as he had back in the Star days. Also a factor was that the Johnsons lived in a very beautiful part of the countryside, in the area where we ourselves now live. We enjoyed visiting them and the six of us remained close. We would have dinners, go places and hang out together.

From early on I possibly got on better with Peter than with Jo – very likely because Peter talks so much. It's easy to get close to him while Jo is a little quieter. Also Gary and Peter were in close contact and I was always kept up to date with Peter's movements. It came as something of a shock when I heard that Peter and Jo had broken up. I was very sorry for both of them and I remember thinking that Peter was probably more to blame than Jo.

Subsequently Peter took up with a girl who did not fit in well with the old friends' club of the Johnsons, Gary and I. Although I was invited to meet this girl for lunch once, she didn't turn up. Peter Johnson and Gary, without being too disloyal to Peter, did roll their eyes and say sarcastically, 'You missed a right treat there.'

They obviously did not approve of her. As it happens I never did get to meet any of the girlfriends who paraded through Peter's life after he and Jo finished their long relationship, which had been going on for some eight years.

Instead I would be fed reports about what nightmares they all were and how Peter had no idea of what he was really looking for in a woman.

Gary and I finally split in the late 1980s. We had been down that road many times and yet both of us were really quite devastated by the break-up, which seemed to be permanent.

Gary confided in Peter a lot and our friends the Johnsons stayed in touch with me and invited me to continue visiting. They were most adamant that just because Gary and I had ended our relationship did not mean they were no longer available to me. 'You will always be welcome to come up and stay,' they said generously on more than one occasion.

Taking them at their word, I arranged to go and stay with them. Peter had been in London visiting friends and offered to give me a lift back up to Shropshire at the end of a weekend. That was the beginning of us having a closer relationship. It was a time of interminable sessions during which he would set out intending to listen to all my troubles, but in fact spend the entire journey talking about his girlfriends and continuing anguish over failed relationships. I can't remember the exact point when I decided that he needed taking in hand or he was just going to throw away his life. He needed me to manage his life properly and sort him out once and for all.

Peter had changed jobs a few times over the years since he had been on the Shropshire Star and he and Jo had bought a house together. The property was now on the market and his great dream was to go to America and travel. Having a great love of so many types of American music from blues to jazz to rock, he planned to undertake a trip of musical homage to cities like Nashville and New Orleans as well as places associated with American films in which he had a particular interest.

Naturally enough, because I lived in America, I gave him advice as to how to go about it and helped him plan his itinerary. As the time of his trip approached we grew ever closer. Still good friends, we were hovering around more intimate possibilities. I invited him out to stay with me in New York knowing myself how intimidating it was to arrive in New York alone and friendless. My thinking was that he would appreciate some time to recover from the jet lag before he set off travelling. As things happened, Peter arranged to travel back to New York with me after I'd been over in England for a week's break at half-term. This would help him deflect any problems he might have with US Immigration because the authorities are not too keen on people coming to the States as long-term tourists without having anywhere to stay. It seemed more respectable if he'd come to stay with me rather than as a bum of no fixed abode hitching around America.

In the event, he came to New York and was most reluctant to leave my apartment and go travelling. Perhaps inevitably the romance then started.

After we had become lovers, he did actually go off on his musical tour but he kept coming back to New York. It was clear that we were having a more *and more serious relationship and we fell more and more in love as we enjoyed living a life together in the excitement of eating, drinking and socialising in New York.*

Much as I enjoyed the campus life in America, the idea of moving back to England began to take shape in my head in the process of applying for a green card – having lost eligibility for a student green card – it occurred to me that I'd now lived and worked in the States for seven or eight years. Accepting the green card and staying at Columbia would have meant that I'd permanently emigrated to America – and that wasn't my intention, much as I loved it there.

My parents were getting too frail to travel to the States. They had come out for a long visit while I was at Columbia but they didn't feel in good enough health to make the journey again. Inevitably I was restricted to the times I could go home and the difficulty of getting home quickly in an emergency began to worry me.

Peter was sure fairly early on that for him the relationship was serious and he actually asked me to marry him on about date two. I would go along with the emotion of the situation and then have failures of nerve. Partly because it would involve such upheaval for me. My life was good and I loved working at

Princeton, my apartment in New York and a varied and exciting social life.

Of course we had discussed Peter staying in America but the practicalities were not as simple as we would have liked to make out. Though I was ready to go back to England, I did feel I would regret the life I'd be giving up. If the truth be told, I wasn't completely over the breakdown of the relationship with Gary, though I tried to put a brave face on it. I was still very emotionally vulnerable.

My father then had yet another stroke and so I was torn in different directions at once. Still, we started house-hunting in Shropshire and found a beautiful cottage in the countryside overlooking hills. That settled us down. Doubts and questions of the 'Are we doing the right thing?' kind of evaporated. Our fate was sealed.

Peter arrived in New York in November 1989 and we had been seeing each other on and off that previous summer. He returned to England around April 1990. By June, I had followed him over on a year's sabbatical and I lived in London with a friend of mine from Cambridge days, Robert Jones.

Most weekends Peter and I got together in either London or Shropshire and also took several holidays together. By the end of 1990 we were established as a couple.

Peter had proposed to me in New York with an unusual lack of imagination. He chose his moment after he had taken me to see Almodovar's Tie Me Up! Tie Me Down!. The film was all about the horrors of heterosexuality and to take someone to see that film and then say, 'Will you marry me?' showed a distinct lack of judgement.

During my year's sabbatical I worked at the British Library doing research. Most weekends I would make the journey to the Midlands to visit Peter in a miserable little flat he rented in Telford, a new town and not my favourite place.

Still, I set aside my dislike of the place to be with him. But we had a lucky break. In the late spring of 1991 our old friends Peter and Sue Johnson told us they had decided to make a pilgrimage to the shrine at Santiago de Compostela in Spain. They were going to resign their jobs and cycle across Europe. The plan was for them to be away three or four months and would we house-sit for them? We jumped at the opportunity and along with that several other things fell into place.

I had an interview at Sussex University for a position in the English Literature Department and Peter set up his own media business with a friend of his, Richard Slowick, with whom he'd been doing freelance journalism for some years.

We moved into the Johnsons' home in Pentervin, near Minsterley in Shropshire, and while Peter worked in his office in Bridgnorth I would go on long walks. Before I went back to America to teach for a final term at Columbia, we made an offer on the house we loved and were accepted.

Most of my colleagues in New York thought I was deranged to give up America to go back and work in the British educational system. But even for them there was one exception, and the reasons for going to work at the University of Sussex in Brighton were obvious: it was the kind of university that they particularly admired.

The university's intellectual tradition and politics were considered radical and a model of forward thinking. Also the position that was offered at Sussex was closest to the practice of English Literature as I'd been presenting it in America. My feeling was that a British university would be even more true to the essence of my subject.

The teaching staff at Sussex already included some good friends and colleagues. I was familiar with their work and what they were about academically. Sure enough, when I got the job there I did find it very congenial.

On 15 February 1992 we moved into our new home and six months later we were married in

Shrewsbury Cathedral. To me there had never been any doubt that when I got married it would be in the Catholic Church. I don't remember asking Peter's opinion, but he certainly didn't raise any objections. He follows no religion and his mother was Jewish.

Chapter Thirteen

Loved by All

Siobhán was tremendously well regarded by her colleagues in the academic world both in Britain and America. She travelled extensively and throughout the 1990s was in great demand as a guest lecturer at universities in America, Canada and Europe, including both her native Northern Ireland and the Irish Republic, and as a conference speaker.

News of her death shocked and saddened those people who had known of her brave struggle against cancer in 2000. Somehow they began to feel she was invincible and would probably beat the disease again.

Being men and women of letters, their personal written memories of Siobhán hold a special poignancy. Teachers and students alike have offered invaluable contributions to Siobhán's story; this in turn seems to have helped those closest to her to come to terms with her passing.

Siobhán's colleagues were moved to paint unique and fascinating glimpses of her at various stages of her academic career. With their permission, we reprint some of these personal recollections here.

Almost Certain
Dr Jayne Lewis, Professor of English, University of Southern California

One of the more consoling things anyone has ever said to me is that there may be no such thing as calories. The person who said this was Siobhán. Her exact words were: 'I don't believe in calories. Almost certainly there are no such things.'

The reader, if female, will immediately understand why it might come as a relief to hear these words from anyone. It was, however, a particular relief to hear them from Siobhán because this meant that possibly they could be believed. And if what she said were not the truth, it was at least as Siobhán once said of her husband Peter's music: 'With respect to art, it's the next thing to it.'

To Siobhán, it seems, a surprising range and

number of things were almost certain. Prince Charles having cleared out of Ludlow Castle by the time we hoped to visit it. The celebrated author Philip Pullman having sat beneath the same tree in Oxford where she and Constance and I settled ourselves on the last day we ever spent together.

Her mother, Belfast suddenly behind her, missing her enemies more than she did her friends. Tony Blair – or Prince Charles, for that matter – turning out to be other than what he appeared to be. 'Almost certainly,' Siobhán would say to each of these possibilities. No elaboration was required. Betrayal was almost certain, as were conflict, and defeat. But so was the beautiful meeting of unlike things. So were a hundred versions of what is commonly called love.

It is all but impossible to imagine a time when I did not know Siobhán. It is equally difficult to be certain that I actually did. What is hardest to picture, though, is anyone more constant, or more mysterious, or anyone in whom, if not whom, it has consequently been more possible to believe.

Siobhán divides my own life in two, my having met her exactly half of it ago. That would have been during her first spring at Princeton. She was a graduate student there, as I would be myself in a few months' time and she had, surely by chance, been assigned to be my guide around the campus on the day I visited. We were to begin with her medieval literature seminar.

This particular seminar was taught in the library basement by someone across whose front porch steps we'd later (much later) consider stringing a length of steel wire – at neck level, Siobhán would specify, and very tight. This was actually a fine medievalist, a fine man, but he would be giving me a Fail on my Latin translation exam and Siobhán was nothing if not loyal. Of course, no one truly wanted anything in the way of revenge to be taken upon him. It was just a thought.

When Siobhán introduced herself that first day – months before the steel-wire plot, minutes before her medieval seminar began – I repeated her first name wrong.

Americans, when they pronounce this name, tend to push the 'Av' sound in the middle over into an 'Ab'. I knew of a character on an American soap opera, the only Siobhán I'd heard of up until then, whose name was consistently mangled in this way. The important thing is that Siobhán, the real Siobhán, did not correct me. Whether this was out of tact in the face of my awkwardness or pity for my provincialism I will never know, though I am almost certain it was never held against me.

It turns out that 'Siobhán' is a female variant of

'John', her father's name. In the beginning was the word. The John of the Christian Gospels is a man of declarations but also of mysteries. He is a fool for love, and an idealist to the core. On the other hand, Siobhán saw her surname, Kilfeather, as the work of history's tarry brush, of an English occupation that had taken aim at the Irish Gilfedder and vowed to blot it out. When Constance was born, Siobhán returned that original name to her, but she kept Kilfeather for herself, admitting the mixture that was in it, the marks of complexity and history, of difference from her child and even from herself.

As I think of all of this, I become more certain that she never held my initial mistake about her Christian name against me. The furious purity of her own principles notwithstanding, she would concede that most things end up sullied and compromised.

On this point – the point of deracination, really – someone once brought up the kidnapping of Jonathan Swift. As is relatively well-known, Swift's nurse had stolen him when he was a small child. She had taken him to England. What was Siobhán's view on this event? Her view could be summarised in a very few words. 'Yes,' she murmured, as from afar. She was pregnant with Constance at the time and had wrapped herself in a spotted coat. 'And how can we be sure it's Swift that we got back again?'

Many are tormented by the question of how anyone can be sure of anything. Entire careers – Swift's literary one to some extent included – have been built upon this mote in the human eye. I don't know that the question of certainty especially troubled Siobhán, however. I believe she took its inscrutability well in her stride.

All the same, at Princeton she was a student of the age of Swift, which she hoped would be known one day as the age of an Irish woman writer named Mary Davys. So far, she was doing a fine job of making all but certain that this would occur. Mary Davys had written a book called *The Merry Wanderer*. Siobhán was writing about her writing of this book, but bore no grudge against those of us who had never heard of it before.

Her second year at Princeton, the year she began working seriously on Mary Davys, was my first. We both lived in the graduate college, she in a wing whose sloping wooden floors and baroque eaves, the strategic slant of light through whose mullioned windows, were all part of the university's general aspiration to the Cambridge style. I can't help but wonder what it must have been like for Siobhán to find herself in this too often monstrous approximation of a place to which she had once belonged.

In between calm assertions that she did not believe

in calories – so why not have the slice of cake? – she would tell me so much about Cambridge that I all but dreamed of it myself: the May Ball; the students housed in alphabetical order around a winding corridor. This chance distribution of names had given her the dearest friends of her life, their surnames all clustering around hers in the middle of the English alphabet.

On occasion, one of these particular friends would turn up in Princeton. They were all so stylish and yet so unmannered, so tender-hearted in spite of their wit. Otherwise, I must say, they seemed very unlike Siobhán. I don't believe she ever chose anyone for the resemblance to herself, or that she would have done so even if there were anyone who truly resembled her in the first place, which of course there was not.

Nonetheless, from time to time she would go back to England and her British friends would close around her again. She would disappear from our view. 'Sentimental about nothing but her friends,' one of her American ones once said of her. Almost certainly, I say. Though there may have been more than the single exception. What of Mary Davys, for example? Siobhán herself was another merry wanderer, far from home. She had made those Cambridge friends far from yet another home.

She had, of course, a great many friends at Princeton as well. There were more of them than any one of us could count, or even know about. Two had the use of a stranger's house one summer. It was an enormous house, with a swimming pool out back. Some of us drove out one afternoon. 'I have a need of a swim,' Siobhán announced, right away. Her bathing suit was unusually heavy and dark; she had draped a big towel over her shoulders. When she shrugged it off and slipped into the bright water, asking that to cover her instead, more need was fulfilled than the simple one of a swim. Later, after she told me about the melanoma, I remembered her need for cover, her evasion of impertinent light. Years later Siobhán had finished with Princeton. She had been to Columbia. She had married Peter and she taught at Sussex now. Weekly she travelled all those miles from the quiet hills of Shropshire down to Brighton. As was usual in summer, I found myself in between these two opposing points, which is to say in London; I was to phone the Shropshire farmhouse from Euston Station. I was to say when I would arrive for the weekend we'd planned to spend together. So I phoned once, then twice, a third time even, but there was never any reply, only Siobhán's inexpressibly beautiful voice on the answering machine.

Away? In Germany? But what of me and my train?

The sea of Euston closed over me; it took me down. But no need: I opened them on Siobhán herself, and her black Labrador Ken. She could not have been farther from Germany, though she could easily have forgotten to remove the holiday announcement from her answering machine. But she'd been almost certain, she said, that she would find me where I was. She brought me to Brighton with her – I had never seen it before nor will, I think, again – then back to Shropshire on the night train. Ken was more than half her size, and not adept at handling moving stairs, so when we passed through Euston, Siobhán carried him in her arms.

Once I met Siobhán and Ken in Dublin. Constance's christening was the reason that all of us were there: Peter, Peter's parents, Siobhán's German friend Dorothea [von Mucke]. Constance herself, thank God. On my way to meet them, there was a cab driver sufficiently affable to entertain the question that Siobhán so often brought to mind: 'The luck of the Irish: is that good or bad?' 'It's luck,' was all he would say, which turns out to be all you need to know.

At Siobhán's funeral, there was little talk of luck, though the spectre of the bad kind, the thread-of-precious-life-snipping kind, hovered in the background. Explicit mention was however made of her faith. I believe it was the priest, Father Jonathan Mitchell, who made it. You would expect that. Few if any were entirely certain what he meant by it.

Siobhán had once climbed the steps of Lourdes on her knees, and she had died in what is called the bosom of the church. I had gone to mass with her one summer day in Shropshire, the car she'd been determined to learn to drive plunging madly down all the green and narrow country lanes until it found the tiny chapel buried among trees. I had seen her drop all the money she had with her into the collection box. Still, it is not possible to fill in the contents of her faith, its articles.

That is probably just as it should be. The Catholic liturgy of burial itself, like the Anglican one, falls silent upon such matters, no doubt deliberately. In this same liturgy, however, reference is made to sure and certain hope. In light of that, all of the graves in Hope Common, including Siobhán's, look to the east. I am almost certain that they do.

She Was So Bright

Dr Judith Hawley, Siobhán's colleague at Columbia University and now Senior Lecturer in English, Royal Holloway, University of London

Siobhán is still so vivid to me and I have so many

wonderful memories of her that it is hard to select something to record. But these are the memories and impressions that are currently uppermost, fragments of a wonderful, brave, fiercely intelligent and strong woman.

I will always feel grateful to her because Phil and I got engaged in her apartment in New York when she was teaching at Columbia. We were all watching a rented video of *400 Blows*. Siobhán drifted off to sleep and Phil and I drifted away and decided to get married. So she was the first to know. She was always very supportive of us as a couple, and even more so when we had Olivia.

Her love and generosity were boundless. Her heart was big enough to take in an endless number of people and animals. She devoted herself to her family uncomplainingly. She never asked us as guests to earn our supper, but always provided for us.

I will always admire and envy her for her glamour. Once she wore a beautiful silk ball gown and huge beaded accessories for a simple supper. She could transform herself in seconds. One moment she would come in from taking the dogs for a walk in her wellies and anorak, next moment she would swirl a scarf around herself, put on some bright jewellery and look quite a star.

She had an amazing ability to transform things.

You know how easy it is to mess up a house. She seemed to let mess build up quite happily if people were enjoying themselves, then whisk through a room, put things back in order, place a vase on a table and all was different.

Her laugh, her tone of voice, the turn of her hands gave such energy and meaning to her utterances.

I am so glad that she found contentment with Peter and that she took such pride and pleasure in Oscar and Constance. She amazed me with her ability to combine her love for her family and her intellectual drive. She was so bright in so many ways.

I miss her.

To the Children
Carol Barash PhD, Siobhán's fellow student at Princeton 1983–7

Dear Constance, Oscar and Peter,
When I first heard that your mom had died, I sat down to remember all of the things she had done in the short time I knew her as a fellow graduate student and friend at Princeton.

I felt a great calm, and sensed a bird soaring in open light. 'Siobhán's spirit,' I thought, as the bird soared higher and higher. She seemed very calm and content. When I told this story to the friends gathered in Shrewsbury, two different people said, 'It must have been a heron.'

It is fitting that your mother would send an image like this, between and among people, as she connected us all the time, with the intense beauty of her vision, the powerful metaphors she read and wrote and gave meaning as she shared them with others.

I want you to know and remember that nothing made your mom happier than the two of you. She used to send me drawings that Constance made, and she told me of Oscar's sense of humour. She was so proud of you both, and asked for the miracle of health to get to know you more, love you more. Though it feels like her life was horribly short – and it was – I also know she was granted a miracle of seven extra years to get to know you two, to love you as only a mother can. You will have that love for ever.

I lost my father when I was young, from cancer too, and I know how very painful it can be. In the days and weeks and years to come, there may be moments that feel almost unendurable. And yet, I can tell you, these moments pass, and the glowing spirit of a good person, a loving mother and friend, lives on. You will have these memories for ever.

You knew your mother in the details of everyday life – the simplest and deepest way one can know another person – her smile, her laughter, her very strong sense of what was right and what was wrong, her vibrant connections to other people. You will have these connections always, and the people who loved your mother will be here for you. We will be here for you in whatever ways you need us, and we will be here for you for ever.

Though I had not seen your mother in many years, I came to see you this week to give back to you my sense of your mother's greatness, her amazing success as a human being, a person who did the right things, who loved people fiercely and with all her being, and with a great tenderness too. I see in each of you bits of your mother's playful spirit and her deep intellect, and I know you will carry forth her spirit in ways that each of you will discover over time.

As you grow up, as you become yourselves day by day, may the memory of your amazing mother be a comfort to you, as her friendship and love were a comfort to you when she was alive, and may you – in honour and memory of your mother – soar on your own wings, knowing that you were loved, and you are loved, exactly as you are. And you are connected to the people your mother knew, the spirit she created among us, by infinite threads of connection that you can draw on for sustenance and support. These invisible but infinite threads remain, and they remain for ever.

Come visit me and my family and we will laugh together.

All love, Carol Barash, PhD

Snow in April

Professor John Archer, former colleague at Princeton, now Director of Graduate Studies, Department of English, New York University

It sometimes snows in April in New York City, and just such a thin squall preceded the phone call from a friend telling me of Siobhán's passing. I can't remember meeting Siobhán – we were part of a circle of friends at Princeton in the Graduate College in the Autumn of 1983. In Princeton, she liked dogs, of course, and all animals, except perhaps, and just at that time, cats. Her first roommate, who did not last long, had a cat named Pookie – let that serve as an explanation. Siobhán herself had a red racing bicycle she called Clytemnestra. On a walk in the nearby woods, the Institute Woods as we called them, a black dog followed her home and reminded her of her old Belfast dog Tarry. The stray was shooed off with a regretful 'go home', but it wasn't long before Doug entered the picture, a black lab–retriever cross picked last out of a litter somewhere in rural Pennsylvania and driven back to New Jersey by a group of us one weekend afternoon.

Doug was around for just a few years but I think his character is sufficiently known. It was Doug who left fleas in the houses of more than one senior faculty member after summer stays. Siobhán loved him dearly.

She was a leader among the graduate students in English, and on a flyer protesting departmental policies she once placed an illustration from a veterinary manual called 'The De-barking of a Dog', which made a point about our lack of representation.

In our later years at Princeton we became fast friends with Hunter and Gayle, playing Pictionary, exploring shady Italian restaurants around Trenton, and watching ridiculous television programmes like *The Equalizer* at their apartment. Siobhán also wrote a path-breaking dissertation on eighteenth-century Irish women and the political novel.

The English department at Columbia University in New York hired seven new people in 1987 and Siobhán and I were both part of this group. A new circle of friends arose, although more slowly and mostly outside that group of seven for one reason or another.

Dorothea and Karen and several other women

gathered around Siobhán, who once again became leader of a band apart. In New York she lived at an apartment in a building on West 112th street and at 39 Claremont Avenue, Apartment 113, close to campus. No dogs entered her life in New York, but she delighted in the strange breeds that inhabited her buildings, like the famous.

An elderly lady at the Claremont Avenue address repeatedly told us that she had once been a leading light in 'the dog game', meaning breeding, the kennel club and the like. 'Slightly ga-ga' was Siobhán's verdict, although it was not an unkindly one.

She enjoyed long walks down Riverside Park, films of all sorts, but maybe especially *Goodfellas*, the Museum of Modern Art and the Metropolitan Museum, the occasional opera (Puccini's *Manon Lescaut* was one), riding on the subway, and endless conversations with friends. Her parents visited during the early years in New York, and so did Robert and, later, Liane. Siobhán's favourite places to shop were the Upper West Side and SoHo as it then was. She supported a wide variety of students, especially Joe and Elaine, and was befriended by Edward Said, Marcellus Blount and other colleagues in the department.

People at Columbia were surprised and truly sad when she left. But she never felt at home in New

York or in America, and she believed that home was something she had to create. It was as if she was in exile from the future she knew was about to happen.

When the April snow and the phone call came, I was reminded of a moment, about seventeen years ago, when a sudden snow flurry hit the south-east corner of Sixth Avenue and Houston Street as Siobhán and I were walking back from a movie at Film Forum. She had made the decision to return to Britain for good.

'That's the way life is,' she turned and said to me with a smile. 'It's New York, and it starts to snow, it's beautiful and you thought you'd be here for ever.' She allowed cheerfully and with courage for tales of the unexpected and, worse sometimes, of the expected. I'll miss her very, very much.

The Meaning of Life
Obituary in the Selwyn College Calander by close friends Liane Jones and Rachel Wilshaw

People who remember Siobhán Kilfeather (Selwyn 1976–9) will be saddened to hear that she has died much too young, aged forty-nine. Siobhán came up to Selwyn in 1976 as one of the college's first generation of women undergraduates. It was no accidental choice: Siobhán liked to break new ground and appreciated the fact that Selwyn was one of the first men's colleges to go co-residential.

She made an immediate impression on many of us. Born and brought up a Belfast Catholic, she had a soft Irish voice, sharp tongue and daring wit. (She also stood out because in a sea of mid-70s denim, she arrived wearing a tweed suit, her mother's tip for blending in with the English.)

She had a deep love for her subject, English Literature. She would sit quietly in seminars and group classes, listening to others, and then voice thoughts that made us blink with their incisiveness and originality. She was already dauntingly well-read.

We were aghast to find she had actually completed all the recommended pre-course reading, perhaps helped by the fact that she knew all of Jane Austen by age eleven and most of George Eliot and Tolstoy by about sixteen. Going to Dublin with her at the end of our first year was a revelation as she supplied an endless stream of literary facts and anecdotes.

Siobhán's many friends remember her as clever, quixotic and fun, with a strong sense of duty at her core. Particularly memorable for us were the long conversations, which would start with that week's essay subject and lead seamlessly on to intense discussions about culture, society and the meaning of life. At Cambridge she was active in left-wing politics, trying out many points on the spectrum from Labour to Trotskyism.

She loved polemic and could never encounter a point of view without challenging it. She was also involved in voluntary work, journalism, JCR politics and amateur dramatics and had her full quota of parties and emotional trauma.

Her love of literature remained central throughout. Siobhán always said she was lucky to have been taught by Dr Wil Sanders and Dr Jean Chothia. The value they placed on the individual's response to writing stayed with her; when she became a university teacher herself she would pass on the gift.

Siobhán left Selwyn with a 2.1 and spent a disorganised, eventful couple of years in Rome and Belfast before embarking on an academic career. She won a Fulbright Scholarship to do a PhD at Princeton University in America, then taught at Columbia University, where she revelled in being at the cutting edge of literary theory, where scholarly controversies abounded.

She became an authority on eighteenth-century Irish literature, while also teaching and writing on the Gothic, romantic literature, post-colonialism and gender studies. Among students she had a reputation as an inspiring, imaginative teacher who would get them thinking outside the academic box, by the scruff of the neck if necessary. Many of them also discovered her kindness and loyalty. Siobhán published critical editions of Maria Edgeworth and Louisa M. Alcott, but will perhaps be best remembered in literary circles as an editor of *The Field Day Anthology of Irish Writing*. She worked on Volumes IV and V, which sought to represent women's contribution to Irish culture. Characteristically, Siobhán argued that they should include men's writing alongside women's, on the basis that being male did not disqualify them from shedding interesting light on the subject.

The volumes were published in 2002, by which time Siobhán had returned to England and was living happily with her husband Peter Jameson and their two much wanted and loved children, Constance and Oscar. For twelve years she combined a home life in rural Shropshire with lecturing at Sussex University (a challenging commute) until in 2004 she took a post at Queen's University and the family moved to Belfast.

For Siobhán it was a return to her roots and, to an extent, her religion. A few weeks after organising a fiftieth birthday party for Peter, she discovered that the melanoma she had battled against in the 90s had returned, this time spreading fast and mercilessly.

She died in unseasonably beautiful weather on Easter Saturday.

Siobhán Marie Kilfeather, born 9 August 1957; died 7 April 2007.

Heaven Will Not Be Wanting
Elise MacAdam, Siobhán's student at Columbia

I met Siobhán when I was at an especially impressionable age at an especially impressionable moment. It was my first year of college and nothing made it more clear that I didn't know much about anything than bumbling into her class. It was a survey of eighteenth-century literature, daunting because of the rumours (all true) that her courses involved having to become intimate with extremely long books. Those books, but more to the point, Siobhán, changed everything for me.

In the first place, Siobhán was splendid. Her interests and the power she had to trigger those passions in other people were irresistible, and I remember so clearly how much I wanted to follow her path, but being daunted by her intelligence and her rarely repressed scepticism. Even when I was eighteen I had a feeling that she was difficult to impress, which was one reason I was surprised by the first non-school exchange I had with her. It was a Monday and she asked how my weekend had been. I said I had been to a party and couldn't figure out why I had exerted myself flirting badly with someone who was really pretty dopey. Siobhán's reply cut through this adolescent pondering: 'At least you didn't wake up in some strange bed with a dolt.'

It is hardly worth mentioning that she was right.

It didn't matter that I couldn't tell if she was chiding me or genuinely accentuating the positive. That chat made me want to have her as a friend. And she was.

Siobhán became a compass for me. For a long time she was my teacher and with her I learned more than my friends now want to hear about the literature and politics of England and Ireland in the eighteenth and nineteenth centuries. More fundamentally, though, she showed me how to think, how vital it is to look for irony at every opportunity, that one should tune in to the things left unsaid in every circumstance – literary or across a dining table – since the unspoken is often more significant than whatever people are pretending to talk about. She taught me sympathy and subtlety and showed me how to be myself.

It is hard not to be aware of the irony that memorialising someone means talking a lot about oneself, but I hope that these things I say convey how deep Siobhán's friendships ran, what a force she was in her friends' lives. After she left Columbia University and Manhattan, to reside in Shropshire ('Michael Powell country,' she told me – *Gone to Earth* was set in and filmed there) I saw Siobhán infrequently but that never interrupted our conversations.

One of Siobhán's great charms for me is that she never shied away from any kind of conversational horror. In some ways she embraced it. Perhaps this is part of how rigorously honest she always was, but I always found her willingness to discuss the uncomfortable incredibly reassuring. All of the 'petty little daily humiliations' as she described them that cropped up in Jane Austen's stories were just as horrible and amusing to her when they happened in real life. She is the one friend who would welcome tales of workplace indignities, frets about the gore of childbirth, intricate transgressions on the part of family members – everything was permitted and the more egregious the story, the more rewarding was her response.

Having children is particularly on my mind these days because I had my second one quite recently. I was very nervous about whether or not to become a mother, let alone a mother twice over. Siobhán never tossed me the standard line, the way most people with spectacular children do, about how everyone who is a parent loves it. Instead of attempting to debunk my angst, Siobhán took it seriously and treated it with her usual toughness, while encouraging me to give motherhood a go. She did the same thing a second time around. When I told her I was pregnant with another son, she pointed out that names would be a problem since I had surely used my favourite boy's name on my first child. This was true. I couldn't think of any name I liked better than Felix (my older boy's name) and, as Siobhán mentioned, it wouldn't do to have a transparently second-best name for a second son.

In this, Siobhán helped me as she did in every tricky decision I have had since I was an undergraduate. In keeping with Jewish tradition, my son's name was inspired by Siobhán's first initial. He is Sebastian. I planned to honour her this way for months but being superstitious I wanted to tell her after he was born. Sadly, I waited too long. Sebastian's birth only deepens his connection to Siobhán. I was unable to attend her funeral in Shropshire because Sebastian was born, that very day, 19 April, during the event itself. Having a baby is not for the faint of heart and Siobhán was in the front of my mind as Sebastian was brought into the world.

When it comes to Siobhán, words fail me. I don't know what I will do without her guidance and humour, interest and rigour. I can't even describe how wonderful she was without relying on another movie by Michael Powell, *A Matter of Life and Death*. When Marius Goring, playing a foppish fellow whose job it is to conduct souls to heaven arrives on Earth, he caresses a flower saying: 'One is starved for Technicolor up there.'

With Siobhán, heaven will not be wanting. It will have Technicolor with all three strips, super saturation, dazzling hues.

And I am jealous.

SIOBHÁN'S STORY: JUST CALL ME 'PROFESSOR'

It seems that the wedding plans took some people by surprise and more so in relation to Peter than me. People would ask our reasons for choosing to go down the aisle in a Catholic cathedral. Half joking and half serious, he would relay to them the explanation I had rehearsed with him.

I think it rather took people aback when we pointed out that the alternative would have been to get married in a registry office and surely no one would think I had such regard for the British Government that I would allow the state to tell me the terms of my marriage.

I would rather not be married at all than have a

piece of paper endorsed by a police state. Surely if you wanted to make a formal commitment and uphold sacred vows it should be a religious service in front of friends and family in a place of worship.

Many people, especially in the family, were shocked that during the wedding service Peter and I exchanged paintings rather than gold rings and I admitted that I had no intention of using the name Jameson. To be honest, it never occurred to me to change my name.

Among my contemporaries in America, the last couple I knew where the wife had changed her name was in about 1980 and even then they admitted it was rather socially embarrassing to have done it. Most of my women friends had professional careers and it just wouldn't have occurred to them to change their names.

There was one instance where a couple had both changed their names. They amalgamated their surnames and hyphenated them. Peter and I gave a passing thought to Jameson-Kilfeather but it was never really an option that appealed to either of us.

As for the wedding rings, that concerned an idea that I had at the time. One thing I didn't like about getting married was a suggestion that marriage was the assumption that married people in some way occupied a more central position in society.

The problem I had with rings was not the symbolism of wholeness, which I approve of, but again the implied suggestion that married people were somehow privileged. Indeed I do have a wedding ring that has been in my family for generations. I wear it sometimes, though it is tight for me. It had belonged to my great-grandmother, my grandmother, my Auntie Jean and then my mother gave it to me along with her wedding ring. However, I objected to the idea that people put rings on their fingers declaring, 'I'm married now,' and everyone must know I am a married woman.

In the cause of equality it was suggested that perhaps men should wear a ring too. But that didn't resolve the issue as far as I was concerned. You can always tell the married man who has slipped his wedding ring into a pocket the minute before he was introduced to you.

I didn't feel comfortable with those outward symbols or feel the need to try to ensure Peter's fidelity by making him wear a ring. Another issue which troubled me was that lots of my friends are gay and lesbian and even in a committed relationship they are not entitled to that positive endorsement [the law allowing same-sex civil ceremonies was introduced in 2006] so I rejected the ring symbolism as expressed in our society. As for the name business, I had no problem with being called Miss or Mrs because I prefer to be known as Professor Kilfeather.

Children were very high on our agenda and though to us they were not a reason for getting married, they were a firm part of our relationship together. Peter and I started trying to have children before the wedding – so even by the time we got married we were aware that it was not going to be easy for me to conceive.

It happened that my closest friend had suffered infertility problems and had tried out some possible treatments. Having been aware of her experience, it encouraged us to act earlier than we might have done.

Many people wait several years to seek help but we felt after a year of making an active effort to conceive that we should have had some success. Peter agreed that we should go for a series of investigative tests.

The results produced some suggestions but not totally conclusive reasons for the infertility. There wasn't a single obstacle but the experts thought a combination of factors were leading to a low sperm count. Age could be a factor as we were both over thirty-five. I had a laparoscopy which showed slight traces of cystic ovaries and I also had a history of irregular ovulation. More treatments were undertaken at the Shrewsbury Nuffield Hospital, including biothermy, which is a heat treatment on the lining of the womb. Various drug treatments were also prescribed.

We had been consistently if not obsessively trying to conceive for about six months before we got married in 1992. After the wedding we both became quite obsessive about our desire for a baby.

The World Cup in 2004 acted as a trigger, probably because it stimulated and excited us both so much. Before Brazil beat Italy in the final, Constance was conceived – just a month before we had decided to begin our final IVF treatment.

Also our savings had been set aside for the procedure because we knew it was very expensive. We were over the moon when I conceived Constance naturally and even more delighted when she was born a perfectly healthy and beautiful baby with red hair like her dad and blue eyes like her mum.

There was a repeat performance when we began to try for a second baby. This time we sought advice and guidance straight away. Peter and I hoped that, having successfully delivered Constance, the problem had been resolved, but the consultant informed us that this wasn't always the case.

We embarked on treatment that involved me going to the hospital every day and the doctor looking to see how the egg was growing. In the month Oscar was conceived they would show me pictures. When he grows up, I can tell him that I saw him when he was still an egg, even before the sperm had fertilised the egg.

My father lived to see Constance born and my mother lived to see our family complete with two children – one girl, one boy and a set of contented parents.

I remember very clearly the last time that my father saw Constance. Peter and I were due to go to Ireland just after Christmas year but we all got a very bad dose of flu. We had rented a cottage near my parents and were due to drive over taking the dogs and the plan was to have a carefree family holiday visiting grandparents and family. However, when it came to the day we were all too ill to go. Rather than let my parents down completely, it was agreed that I would fly over with Constance. I stayed just two nights so that my parents could spend some time with her in their own home. My father spent the whole time just doting on her and the night before our departure he did not go to sleep at all. Waking several times in the night, I realised that my father had spent the whole night just standing in the doorway watching Constance asleep in my arms. He thought his grand-daughter was great. He really fell *in love with her. That visit was the last time we saw my father alive.*

I wasn't with my father when he died at home in Ireland. The phone call came in the middle of the night letting me know that he had died. He suffered a fatal heart attack while watching Question Time on television. On his death certificate it says 1 March but it was actually 29 February 1996. Knowing my father I like to think that he died in a paroxysm of rage at some outrageous statement, probably something that David Dimbleby had said. What we do know is that he asked my mother for a drink and she went to the kitchen to get him water. By the time she came back, he had already suffered a heart attack. The ambulance was called and although they spent some time trying to revive him, my mother insists that he was already dead before the ambulance arrived. He would have liked to die on a day like 29 February because it's special and we only have to remember the anniversary every four years.

My mother came to live with us in Shropshire after my father died. It was difficult in many ways because she missed lots of things about Ireland and insisted on going back and forward frequently. She found it very difficult to adjust to living with a family with two young children.

I found it difficult because she smoked. I hated it around the children and the whole situation made me very tense. Like a great many mother-and-daughter attempts to live together, I suspect, she thought everything I cooked was ghastly. At the dinner table she would sit and pick at her food until I would give in and cook the food she liked. To be honest, Peter liked it as well, things like lamb chops, potatoes and peas every night. But I hated it and this constant unease over food made for a miserable time.

We had a lot of irritation and tension with each other – but I think often that is what it is like in families when several generations try to live together. Of course, I blame myself and think that I should have been more understanding. At seventy she was grieving for my father after forty-six years of marriage. She was very badly shocked by his sudden death and in poor health herself.

One thing I am eternally grateful for is that both my parents lived to see the ceasefire in Northern Ireland. This lifted a great strain from them and filled them with hope for the future of the country.

Like so many other families in the thirty years of the Troubles, they had got used to living with the constant violence, the horrors and the overpowering tension in Belfast and other cities of

Northern Ireland. They hadn't realised what a burden would be lifted when life returned to a semblance of normality.

If peace in Northern Ireland gave my father hope, the fall of the Berlin Wall did not please him. I remember him lying in a hospital bed and weeping with sadness and regret that he had lived to see the reunification of Germany. Like many of his generation, he felt the world a safer place with Germany split in two.

Chapter Fourteen

Never to Be Forgotten

Responses of relatives and friends to the sad news of Siobhán's passing:

Oscar Jameson, Siobhán's son, nine
Mummy was nice because she always let everyone's opion [*sic*] count.

Constance Gilfedder, Siobhán's daughter, twelve
I remember the way that my mum always used to sort everything out, like if there was a problem at home or school or work – she would always help people even if it would have been easier for her to ignore the problem. I think that her friends trusted her and knew she would never let people get in trouble if she could help it.

Matthew Hill, musician friend in Shropshire
Siobhán was a real diamond, lighting up rooms and lighting up lives.

**Sara Young, midwife and friend
in Shropshire**
She used to put the fear of God into me with her straightforwardness – but I grew to value it – and now I shall miss it.

Julia Rose, Sara Young's daughter, eight
I like Siobhán because she was kind to me.

Edward Pomfret, Sara Young's son, eleven
Siobhán was a very kind person.

**Bethan Kilfoil, Siobhán's former colleague at
Princeton and now a political journalist for
RTE in Dublin**
I remember going to stay with Siobhán in New York when I had a broken heart – she was so kind, she fed me, listened to me moaning for a week and cheered me up.

Cousin Denise Bradley
Siobhán once said that my mother had been taken from this earth at an early age because she was too

good for it. I think you too Siobhán have gone too soon. Love you.

Cousin Michael Docherty

At many times in my life I remember Siobhán, as a boy, as a teenager, student days (I was so proud when she went to Cambridge) – the family intellectual. My mother's funeral, my wedding – but the abiding memory will be of the brave young woman who taught English in Rome and the lunches we had there. I am glad that I knew her.

Professor Jenny Bourne Taylor, Professor of English at the University of Sussex

Siobhán was the most wonderful colleague at Sussex and we all became great friends. She always had a caustic and witty comment to make about the madness of academic life. I can't believe she is not with us any more.

Dr Margaret Doody, Siobhán's tutor and mentor at Princeton and now Professor of English, Notre Dame University, Indiana, USA

A starry messenger – a bird that flies away.

Dr Dorothea von Mucke, Head of German Department, Columbia University, New York, USA
Siobhán will always be with those of us who have known her. Her capacity to love, to live intensely and think critically.

Cousin Maura Hickey
My first memory of Siobhán was of her standing in front of our fire at 22 Greeve Walk at three years old reciting [W.B. Yeats's] 'The Lake Isle of Innisfree'. We all knew then that Siobhán was no ordinary child.

John McGuckian, Siobhán's fellow student of creative writing at Queen's University, Belfast, and now poet and teacher
Your soul was needed in heaven to save us all. Siobhán was not just generous but practised her generosity; she always *did* something for her friends. She was also egalitarian, so that her generosity was not limited.

If you saw her in action as a teacher you would see this. The same standards that she applied to herself, her family, her friends and her colleagues, she also applied to students.

SIOBHÁN'S STORY: WHATEVER WILL BE

After all the sadness they had endured in their own lives, it would have been absolutely terrible for my parents to know that their only daughter had cancer. Of course there are times when I wish they were still here.

It would be reassuring to be enfolded by the comfort that only a parent can give during these difficult times. I just could not bear to see how devastated they would have been. I think my mother would have fallen to pieces and that my father would have been very profoundly distressed.

I do still believe he would have been a source of moral support to me. He was a very philosophical person about his own illness, though I don't think he could have been the same about mine. No, it was better that they never had to know that I might not get to live a long and healthy life and watch my children grow up after they had gone.

After this pilgrimage to Lourdes, where I have had time to examine my life, I feel a strange sense of calmness. I feel ready to die happy. But I would of course prefer to live happily – if only to stop Peter losing his head and taking up with some totally unsuitable girlfriend.

Over the months of my illness, we have had serious conversations about how the children would be brought up if I were not there for them. We have chosen their guardians very carefully so that there is always a point of reference from someone who knows who I was and the things that I would have wanted for my children.

Though I don't think I can control the children's or Peter's life from beyond the grave, I guess like many other mothers who have been in my situation, my deepest fear is that my husband might form a relationship with someone who did not love my children. I certainly would not ask him not to bring another woman into their lives but I pray that he would make a wise choice. The guardians and other family and friends will hopefully stay close to offer him support and to ensure a continuity with Constance and Oscar's real mother.

However, the fears are not too much to the fore today. I am currently enjoying a great sense of equilibrium and an acceptance of whatever will be, will be. I know that moments like these may not last completely but some of the deep spiritual strength which has been given to me through the visit to Lourdes will undoubtedly see me through the darker times ahead.

It would be too much to expect that I will never fear death or feel bad ever again but there is something here to build on. Generations upon generations of people have not been stupid in treasuring mementoes and relics. In a very real sense this pilgrimage has laid a foundation and when I go into the Royal Marsden for chemotherapy, I know it will help me to have by my bedside rosary beads, holy water and candles from Lourdes. These things will help me recall the immense feelings of strength that I felt in this holy place.

The best I hope for is to maintain my spiritual condition and remember the comfort I experienced.

When I get home I'll tell the children about the story of St Bernadette. However, I would be very wary of telling Constance that people go to Lourdes hoping to be cured. To give the impression that miracles happen would not be fair. I will reinforce the message I have always given her that prayer makes you feel better and special places can make you feel better.

In her winter half-term holiday, I will take Constance to a very lovely place that I visited with my friends Roger and Neil, who live in London and are very spiritual people. For one holiday six years ago, they rented a little Landmark Trust cottage at a place called St Winifred's Well in Shropshire.

This is a holy place and at the time I was unable to conceive a child, they specifically rented the cottage to allow me the chance to bathe in St Winifred's

Well. Subsequently, they take all the credit for Constance coming into being.

Now I want to take Constance to bathe in St Winifred's Well and this will enable me to illustrate to her that Lourdes, where I travelled, is a holy place like St Winifred's Well. Not because these places are magic, but because shrines where others have found or confirmed their faith can help us.

Thank God I have faith.

PARTING WORDS

Since there's not much else I can do for the children now, at least I would like them to believe that we can face these problems in a cheerful and civilised way, and to remember that death is never the worst thing that can happen to a decent person. As long as they have a devoted father, a loving family and good friends they're immensely more privileged than most people in the world. And I know we'll meet again...